Richard Stern

Twayne's United States Authors Series

Frank Day, Editor
Clemson University

TUSAS 625

Richard Stern in 1975.
Photograph courtesy of Elyse Lewin.

Richard Stern

James Schiffer

Hampden-Sydney College

Twayne Publishers ■ New York

Maxwell Macmillan Canada ■ Toronto

Maxwell Macmillan International ■ New York Oxford Singapore Sydney

Richard Stern
James Schiffer

Twayne Publishers
Macmillan Publishing Company
866 Third Avenue
New York, New York 10022

Maxwell Macmillan Canada, Inc.
1200 Eglinton Avenue East
Suite 200
Don Mills, Ontario M3C 3N1

Library of Congress Cataloging-in-Publication Data

Schiffer, James
    Richard Stern / by James Schiffer.
    p. cm. – (Twayne's United States authors series; TUSAS 625)
    Includes bibliographical references and index.
    ISBN 0-8057-4007-4 (alk. paper)
    1. Stern, Richard G., 1928- – Criticism and interpretation. I.
Title. II. Series.
PS3569.T39Z87   1993
813'.54 – dc20   93-10600
                                                          CIP

The paper used in this publication meets the minimum requirements of American National Standard for Information Sciences – Permanence of Paper for Printed Library Materials, ANSI Z39.48-1984.

10 9 8 7 6 5 4 3 2 1

Printed in the United States of America.

For Tanja

Contents

Preface

If in the chapters that follow I offer few judgments about the quality of Richard Stern's writing in relation to that of other writers, one judgment nevertheless informs this study: Richard Stern's stories and novels deserve both a larger readership and more attention from the critical and scholarly establishment. Describing his work in these pages is perhaps a small step toward achieving these two goals.

My first chapter provides a brief overview of Stern's life, surveys his 16 published books, and outlines the important motifs critics have found in his work. Chapter 2 examines Stern's style and also attempts to distinguish, in part on stylistic grounds, Stern's fiction from that of his close friend Saul Bellow. In Chapter 3 I discuss the theme of "geniuses and epigones" in two early novels, *Golk* and *Stitch*. The fourth chapter explores the Americans-in-Europe motif that has fascinated Stern for more than 40 years. In Chapter 5 I look at the comedy of failure, especially in Stern's short stories, while Chapter 6 explores betrayal, both as a subject and as a mainspring of many of Stern's plots.

Chapters 7, 8, and 9 all touch on Stern's practice as an autobiographical writer. Chapter 7 discusses his autobiographical fictions of love as well as his essays about writers who use their own lives as the materials of fiction. Chapter 8 traces the fatherhood theme, which in Stern's fiction has also often drawn on autobiographical sources, especially in the the novella *Veni, Vidi . . . Wendt* (1970) and subsequent works. Chapter 9, on portraiture, examines how Stern fictionally represents the act of capturing others in language and other media. My final chapter discusses Stern's place on the map of contemporary American literature.

Except for reviews of individual books and introductions to a few reissued novels, very little has been written about Stern's fiction. Fortunately, much of the criticism that does exist is of a very high quality, and I have not hesitated to draw heavily from several earlier commentators on Stern's works, especially Peter Buitenhuis, Hugh Kenner, Mark Harris, Bernard F. Rodgers Jr., and Sven Birkerts; I have done my best to acknowledge my debt to these and a number of other insightful critics. Even more frequently, I have called forth Stern's own statements in essays and interviews about his practice as a writer and about the art of fiction generally. I have also been very liberal in quoting from Stern's stories and novels to illustrate important points. Such specimens are, after all, the ultimate reason for a study of this kind. They give readers who do not know Stern's works a taste of his inimitable way with words and remind those who know his work to return to it for renewed pleasure.

Richard Stern has been extremely cooperative in providing material and answering questions, yet he has never tried to shape my opinions in this study or in any other way presume upon our friendship which has now lasted 20 years. Whatever difficulties I have felt as a result of writing about a friend and former teacher have been entirely of my own devising. From studying Stern's life and art I have learned, if nothing else, not to pull punches, not to compromise, not to pander or flatter but rather to be honest in my opinions, even when they are negative. To be anything else, of course, would be a disservice not only to myself but also to Stern.

The interview in the Appendix was first published in the *South Carolina Review* (Spring 1993). Parts of Chapter 1 appeared in a different form in my essay "Richard Stern," in *The Dictionary of Literary Biography Yearbook: 1987*, ed. J. M. Brook (Detroit: Gale Research, 1988). I wish to thank James Atlas for permission to cite and quote from his forthcoming interview with Stern in *Paris Review*; my thanks also go to Hugh Kenner for letting me use a reader report he wrote about one of Stern's manuscripts for a university press. Some of the best commentary on Stern's work can be found in unpublished letters from a distinguished host of writers (Saul Bellow, Lillian Hellman, Tom Rogers, Philip Roth, John Cheever, and others). These letters, many Stern manuscripts, and other items of interest are kept in scores of boxes in the Department of Special Collections at the University of Chicago's Regenstein Library. I am grateful to the librarians there for access to these important papers.

My other acknowledgments begin with Philip Roth who taught a course on Kafka and Bellow I had the pleasure of taking at the University of Pennsylvania in 1972; when Roth learned that I was heading to the University of Chicago for graduate school, he pointed me to Richard Stern. At Chicago I profited from many discussions of Stern's fiction with Brian Stonehill, Bonnie Birtwistle Honigsblum, and Alane Rollings. I am also indebted to several of my colleagues at Hampden-Sydney College who have read Stern's work and shared with me their thoughts about it: Rosalind Hingeley, Hassell Simpson, George Bagby, Jr., and Susan Pepper Robbins. Lawrence Martin, Jr., invited me to give a faculty forum talk on this project. Catherine Pollari and Geraldine Randall, both of Eggleston Library at Hampden-Sydney, provided invaluable assistance in tracking difficult to find bibliographic sources. My gratitude goes as well to Provost and Dean of the Faculty Scott Colley for encouraging me to take a sabbatical in 1990 and to the Professional Development Committee at Hampden-Sydney for awarding me several summer research grants to complete this project. Other friends who have assisted in various Stern ways include Susan Bagby, Steve Shapiro, Deborah Morris, Margarita Barbosa and Leon Bailey, Peggy and David Bevington, and Robin and Marvin Hunt. I would also like to acknowledge the fine work of my editors at Twayne Publishers, especially Liz Traynor Fowler (who left Twayne in 1991), Barbara Sutton, and Sarah McBride, as well as field editor Frank Day of Clemson University. My greatest debt, of course, is to my family: my father and stepmother, Samuel and Dolores Schiffer; my brothers and sisters-in-law Fredric and Mary Jane, Stephen and Michele; and most of all, my son, Toby, and wife, Susan. What I owe to Susan for her help with this project goes well beyond my power to express or repay.

Chronology

1928	Richard Gustave Stern born 25 February in New York City to Marion (Veit) Stern and Henry George Stern.
1940	Graduates from Hunter Model School, New York City.
1944	Graduates from Stuyvesant High School, New York City.
1944-1947	Receives B.A., University of North Carolina, Chapel Hill (Phi Beta Kappa).
1948-1949	Receives M.A. in English, Harvard University (degree offically granted in 1950).
1949-1950	Sails to Europe on the *Queen Mary*; teaches at the Collège Jules Ferry, Versailles, France.
1950	Marries Gay Clark in Paris, 14 March.
1950-1951	Serves as Lektor at the University of Heidelberg. Works as a U.S. Army educational adviser in Frankfurt.
1951	Son Christopher born 20 January 1951.
1952-1954	Enrolled in Ph.D. program in English (and creative writing), University of Iowa.
1952	Daughter Kate born 19 August. First story, "Cooley's Version," accepted by *Kenyon Review*.
1954-1955	Teaches at Connecticut College.
1954	"The Sorrows of Captain Schreiber" is selected for *Prize Stories of 1954: The O. Henry Collection*.
1955	Begins teaching at the University of Chicago in September.
1957	Son Andrew born 19 July.

1960   Publishes *Golk*; wins Longwood Foundation Award for
              "Assessment of an Amateur."

1961   Publishes *Europe: Or Up and Down with Baggish and
              Schreiber*; 24 June, son Nicholas born.

1962   Publishes *In Any Case*.

1962-1963   Is Fulbright Fellow in Italy; meets Ezra Pound in
              Venice.

1963   Wins American Library Association Friends of Litera-
              ture Award for *In Any Case*.

1964   Publishes *Teeth, Dying and Other Matters*.

1965   Publishes *Stitch*; is Rockefeller Fellow.

1966   Publishes *Honey and Wax: Pleasures and Powers of
              Narrative*.

1968   Wins National Institute of Arts and Letters Fiction
              Award.

1969-1970   Teaches at Harvard University.

1969   Meets Alane Rollings in the summer.

1970   Publishes *1968: A Short Novel, an Urban Idyll, Five
              Stories, and Two Trade Notes*.

1970-1971   Teaches at the University of Nice.

1972   Is divorced from Gay Clark Stern in February.

1973   Publishes *The Books in Fred Hampton's Apartment*
              and *Other Men's Daughters*.

1973-1974   Is Guggenheim Fellow; makes trip around the world.

1978   Publishes *Natural Shocks*. Marion Stern dies in July.

1979   Wins Carl Sandburg Award for Fiction for *Natural
              Shocks*. Henry Stern dies in January.

1980   Publishes *Packages*.

1982   Publishes *The Invention of the Real*.

1985   Wins American Academy and Institute of Arts and Letters Medal of Merit for the Novel; marries Alane Rollings 9 August.

1986   Publishes *A Father's Words* and *The Position of the Body*.

1989   Publishes *Noble Rot*.

1990   Wins *Chicago Sun-Times* Book of the Year Award for *Noble Rot*.

1991   Is named Helen A. Regenstein Professor of English, University of Chicago. Sister, Ruth Stern Leviton, dies in August.

1992   Publishes *Shares and Other Fictions*.

Chapter One

Writer's Writer

I do think the idea is to make something very beautiful that's never before existed on earth, something that's very special and moving to people.[1]

When Richard Stern received the first annual Book of the Year Award from the *Chicago Sun-Times* for his 1989 story collection *Noble Rot*, the award citation called Stern "a writer's writer and a complete man of letters."[2] In describing him in this way, members of the selection committee were first of all acknowledging Stern's "generous encouragement" of aspiring writers (Flaherty). More significantly, they were recognizing Stern's distinguished career as a writer – a career that has lasted more than four decades and has thus far resulted in 16 books: eight novels, one novella, five story collections, one anthology of narrative literature, and three "orderly miscellanies" (gatherings of poems, essays, reviews, and autobiographical sketches).[3] Aside from the regularity of their production, what is noteworthy about these books is their fascinating variety, not just of genre but of theme and style. There are also, of course, thematic and stylistic repetitions from work to work, but the main thing that unifies the Stern canon is its author's obvious artistic seriousness. Stern has never compromised his vision.

This unwillingness – and perhaps inability – to compromise has meant that Stern has never reached the best-seller list or enjoyed the popular following of a Tom Clancy or Stephen King, or even the kind that has greeted his two closest literary friends, Saul Bellow and Philip Roth. Given Stern's interest in ideas (many of his protagonists are intellectuals – artists, scientists, academics), this failure to become a household name is not surprising. As Mark Harris has observed, "The complaint has been made of Stern's difficulty, his erudition, or his abstruse vocabulary. In a market system designed for easy reading Stern's voyage has been precarious."[4] Even among sophisticated readers Stern has not always found a receptive audience. In a review of Stern's 1980 story collection, *Packages*, David Kubal explains, "Mr. Stern's lucidity, together with his capacity for affection and the comic, are very rare qualities, shortages in contemporary fiction. The informed reading public, at least, wants its fictive realities uncontaminated by an author's suggestion that human character is greater than its circumstances, or that the condition itself has goodness, or that anyone should be forgiven or tolerated. That Mr. Stern continues to offer these consolations . . . tells us of his artistic integrity."[5]

If Stern has lost some readers by writing to please himself, that same strategy has also gained him many admirers, especially among writers. His work has won praise from Roth and Bellow, of course, but also from authors as diverse as Flannery O'Connor, Anthony Burgess, Tom Rogers, Joan Didion, Norman Mailer, John Berryman, Thomas Berger, Karl Shapiro, and John Cheever. In addition, Stern has held Fulbright, Guggenheim, and Rockefeller fellowships, and his fiction has won numerous awards, including those from the Longwood Foundation, the American Library Association, and the National Council on Arts and Humanities. His novel *Natural Shocks* won the Carl Sandburg Award for Fiction in 1979, and in 1985 Stern received the prestigious Medal of Merit for the Novel from the American Academy and Institute of Arts and Letters. The *Sun-Times* Book of the Year Award for *Noble Rot* came in 1990.

Early Years and Education

Born in New York City on 25 February 1928, Stern grew up on 84th Street and Central Park West (his first home was on 89th and Broadway). His parents were the children of immigrant German-Austro-Hungarian-Jews eager to assimilate into mainstream America. His mother, Marion Veit Stern, had come from a prosperous bourgeois family; pictures from the family album show her in her youth as an accomplished horseback rider. His father, Henry George Stern, was of humbler origins (his father was in the neckwear and accessories business). Although he wanted to be a doctor, Henry became a dentist instead because he lacked the physical strength necessary to climb the several flights of stairs to visit patients. After a rather undistinguished start, he built quite a good practice; for many years he also performed oral surgery once a week at Lenox Hill Hospital. Stern's first memories of narrative pleasure are of listening through the slats of his crib to his father's made-up tales.[6] Though he was an exceptional storyteller, Henry Stern never wrote a word of fiction or autobiography until he was 78. Only then, with the encouragement of his son and his daughter, Ruth Stern Leviton, did he write a brief memoir, *Reminiscences of a Gentle Man*, which his children published privately.[7]

Richard Stern's own brief autobiographical statements indicate that his childhood was sheltered, thoroughly middle class, and reasonably pleasurable, though Stern has also said he was a "terror-stricken child" (Atlas). From an early age books were an important ingredient of life, so important that Stern describes as traumatic the time his mother banned him from the 82nd Street Library because his voracious reading of fairy tales had given him nightmares. The banishment, evidently, did not last long, although Stern did develop an astigmatic crossed eye that required frequent visits to eye doctors and that he had until adolescence; this condition has plagued him again since his late fifties (he has always had red-green color blindness as well). His mother, he reports, thought the crossed eye "a foolish defect in her pomaded wunderkind."[8] Stern implies that his mother's shame bothered him more than the out-of-control eye.

Another source of ambivalence, related to his parents, arose from being Jewish. Stern was not bar mitzvahed, even though he felt he should have been. It was not done in his family; his father did not think the ceremony worth the expense. Instead Stern hid all day in the Paramount Theater, avoiding the friends to whom he later conjured up the synagogue ritual.[9] In college at Chapel Hill five years later he told people he was half-Jewish, "partly to avoid Hillel functions and partly to try [his] luck on the other side of the street" (*FH*, 143). In 1961 Stern wrote that by the time he finished college he had lost most of his "self-conscious embarrassment about Jewishness" (*FH*, 153). By then he had come to take pride in the accomplishments of famous Jewish intellectuals and to enjoy the "slight displacement from ordinary life" that resulted from being an outsider; Jewishness, he wrote in the same essay, was "almost never a factor" in his life (*FH*, 153). Later statements and fictions by Stern, however, suggest that the issue of his Jewishness was and remains more complex than he imagined in 1961 when he was 33.

Stern attended the Hunter Model School in Manhattan (the school was for gifted children – he had to take a test to be admitted), and then Stuyvesant High School. He was a very good student, though not as good in the sciences as a few others in his class who filled the admissions quotas to Ivy and Big Ten schools. Stern's applications to Harvard, Yale, and the University of Michigan were rejected. Fortunately, there was an uncle in Greensboro who encouraged Stern to apply to the University of North Carolina; Stern matriculated at Chapel Hill in 1944. Though his vocation as a writer was more or less determined even before he arrived at UNC, his ambitions were strengthened there by friendships with student-poets Donald Justice and Edgar Bowers. The three friends formed a literary club, at first reading a book each week and later concentrating on their own stories and poems. Bowers and Justice encouraged Stern to write poetry, which he continues to do to this day (one or two poems a year), but Stern concedes that he was not then, and has never been since, in their league as poets (Atlas).[10]

After graduating from UNC in 1947, Phi Beta Kappa key on his watch chain, Stern tried his hand at three jobs – one with a radio station in Florida (evidently, his fiancée's anti-Semitic mother drove him out of town), another with a department store in Indiana, and the third with Paramount Films International (Atlas). These experiences in the work world were a strong inducement to return to the shelter of the academy, this time at Harvard as an M.A. student in English and American literature. While at Harvard he took a fiction-writing course with Albert Guerard and also placed second in the Bowdoin Prize competition with an essay on John Crowe Ransom. Stern enjoyed his time in Cambridge, and in 1969 he returned there to teach in the Harvard summer session. It turned out to be a fateful summer, one that would change his life.

His work for a master's degree completed, Stern sailed for Europe on the *Queen Mary* in 1949. He spent his first year on a Fulbright fellowship in France, teaching English at the Collège Jules Ferry in Versailles. In Paris that first fall he met fellow American abroad Gay Clark, and in the spring of 1950 they were married. The next fall Stern began teaching at the University of Heidelberg; his first child, Christopher, was born there in 1951. Stern describes his experience of being an American (and a Jewish one at that) in postwar Germany as very interesting, often "pleasurable" (*FH*, 153). But landing a steady job proved difficult. After his year in Heidelberg, where he also moonlighted as a cable clerk for the U.S. Army, he and the family transferred to Frankfurt where Stern took a job, again with the army, teaching illiterate soldiers how to read and write. Some of Stern's teaching experiences in Versailles, Heidelberg, and Frankfurt are fondly recounted in the short story "Wissler Remembers."[11]

After three years in Europe, his money almost gone, Stern tried to dream up ways to keep from returning to the United States. While at Harvard he had known a member of the Agnelli family who owned Fiat and therefore wrote to that company asking for work. He wrote also to Winston Churchill, "volunteering to be the Eckermann of his table talk" (Atlas; also *FH*, 141). Neither baited hook drew a nibble, much less a fish. Therefore, with pregnant wife and toddler, Stern headed for Iowa City and the University of Iowa, where he enrolled for a Ph.D. in English literature. In those days there was no Ph.D. in creative writing at Iowa, but Stern was allowed to write fiction for his dissertation. As it is today, the University of Iowa was swarming with writers and writing workshops. His Iowa years, 1952-54, Stern writes, "were big for poets" such as his old friend Donald Justice, Robert Lowell, Don Peterson, Karl Shapiro, Dee Snodgrass, and many others, but he had a number of prose-writing peers as well (*IR*, 136). Stern loved his time there, not so much for Iowa City, which he describes as "*ugggly*," but for his "poet-and-story-writing pals," for whom literature "counted" (*IR*, 137).

During the fall of his first Iowa year Stern received news from John Crowe Ransom that his story "Cooley's Version" had been accepted for publication by *Kenyon Review*; the story appeared in 1954. Stern also published two stories, "The Sorrows of Captain Schreiber" and "After the Illuminations," in *Western Review*, a quarterly journal published by the University of Iowa; both stories would later become chapters in his novel *Europe: Or Up and Down with Baggish and Schreiber*.[12] "The Sorrows of Captain Schreiber" was selected for *Prize Stories of 1954: The O. Henry Collection*.[13] In 1957 Stern edited a special issue of *Western Review* on "American Poetry of the Fifties."[14] The volume featured poems by Justice, Galway Kinnell, James Merrill, W. S. Merwin, Adrienne Rich, Louis Simpson, May Swenson, and several others. Stern also contributed an interview with Norman Mailer to *Western Review* in 1959. The interview, "Hip, Hell and the Navigator," later appeared in Mailer's *Advertisements for Myself.*[15] One other connection between Stern and *Western Review* is worth mentioning: his first exchange of letters with Saul Bellow concerned the journal, which was in serious trouble, and then extinct, by the end of 1959 (Atlas).

Chicago: Years of Achievement

In December 1953 Stern attended the convention of the Modern Language Association, his name on a list of 96 applicants competing for the same job (which went to a candidate from Princeton who was not on the list of 97 [*FH*, 181]). Despite this and other setbacks he was able to find work at Connecticut College, then a women's college, for the 1954-55 academic year. Among his colleagues there were Paul Fussell and Susanne Langer; Langer had recently arrived to chair the Philosophy Department. The next year Stern joined the English Department at the University of Chicago, and he has remained there teaching creative writing and modern literature ever since, except for brief assignments at the University of Venice, University of Urbino, University of Nice, State University of New York at Buffalo, University of California at Santa Barbara, and Harvard. (He has also traveled widely over the years to South America, Africa, Asia, and Australia, as well as to Europe, often on cultural programs sponsored by the U.S. State Department.) Stern has written with great affection about the University of Chicago, that "great Gothic hive of instruction and research" ("Wissler Remembers," *NR*, 274). In 1966 he dedicated his anthology of narrative literature, *Honey and Wax*, to the school.[16] In 1991 the university reciprocated by naming Stern the Helen A. Regenstein Professor of English and General Studies in the Humanities.

From the eyes of a transplanted New Yorker this city by the lake was "a backwash of Eastern tides" (*FH*, 187), but over the years Stern has come to appreciate Chicago's strength, its ethnic diversity, its toughness and its openness. In Chicago, he writes, "I feel that in a small way I count for something" (*FH*, 190). Stern is proud to be associated with such Chicago writers as Sherwood Anderson, Nelson Algren, and Saul Bellow, who have made the city "the setting for excess, rapidity, confusion, gorgeousness, bitter triumph, overreaching, bitter collapse."[17] Teaching at the University and living for more than 35 years in the same Hyde Park neighborhood has given Stern's life a stability that is rare for academics and creative writers in post–World War II America. His two younger children were born in Chicago (in 1957 and 1961), and all four have grown up there. All 16 of Stern's books have been published during these Chicago years.

From 1960 to 1965 five volumes appeared in rapid succession: the novels *Golk* (1960), *Europe: Or Up and Down with Baggish and Schreiber* (1961), *In Any Case* (1962), and *Stitch* (1965), and the story collection *Teeth, Dying and Other Matters* (1964).[18] Though Stern was obviously writing at a rapid pace during this time, the impression of voluminous production (Flannery O'Connor called him "One-a-year Stern" [*FH*, 215]) is misleading since much of what he published in the early sixties was written during the previous decade; two stories in *Teeth, Dying and Other Matters*, in fact, were written in Europe in 1949. Stern wrote much of *Europe: Or Up and Down with Baggish and Schreiber* while he was a graduate student at the University of Iowa in the early fifties. An earlier version of that book – then a collection of stories – served as his Ph.D. dissertation. *Golk* was written in nine months in 1957-58.[19]

In an essay timed to coincide with the Phoenix Press reissuing of *Golk* in 1987, Stern describes the writing of both *Golk* and *Europe*: "When I first published stories in 1953 and '54 (in the *Western* and *Kenyon Reviews*), editors wrote to ask if I were working on a novel. I wasn't, but said I was and started right up. I worked from one of the short stories, 'The Sorrows of Captain Schreiber,' joined it to several others and tried making connections among them. In 1957, I was stuck. Only after I finished *Golk* did I see how to bring off the other book, *Europe: Or Up and Down with Baggish and Schreiber*" ("On *Golk*," 32). One of the inspirations for *Golk* was Allen Funt's television show "Candid Camera," which Stern watched with great enjoyment in New York before it went national (Funt had earlier made movie shorts, and before that he had a radio show called "Candid Mike"). Stern was fascinated by Funt's godlike "gift for discovering the gift and power of 'amateurs' " ("On *Golk*," 31). From this Stern wove a tale of a "Candid Camera"–style show ("You're on Camera") that becomes an overnight sensation, goes national, and in the hands of its genius creator, Golk, begins to expose the corruption of public officials until Golk is fired by network executives and replaced by less talented underlings who betray their mentor.

Golk had been rejected by 18 publishers before it was accepted by Criterion Books, a small house that went under the week the novel appeared in print ("On *Golk*," 32). This misfortune aside, the book was well-received, even nominated for a Pulitzer Prize. The success of *Golk* no doubt helped Stern the next year to publish *Europe: Or Up and Down with Baggish and Schreiber* with McGraw-Hill. The novel traces the mostly comic adventures of three Americans in Europe and also explores the Nietzschean notion that "every man of character has a typical experience which recurs over and over again" (*Europe*, 1). Max Schreiber, a middle-aged lawyer divorced from a wife and daughter in Connecticut, has the repeated experience of being disappointed in love; ex-dry-goods clerk Theodore Baggish meanwhile makes his fortune in Europe while Schreiber's fortunes plummet. In fact, Baggish's success depends on his exploitation of Schreiber. Stern follows also the fate of Robert Ward, a less important character who lives in Europe and then returns to the States essentially untouched by his time abroad.

Whereas *Golk* and *Europe* are comic (though often darkly comic) novels, Stern's third novel, *In Any Case* (1962), is a serious fiction of suspense, espionage, and self-discovery. Samuel Curry, a 57-year-old American expatriate, sets out to clear the reputation of his son, Bobbie, who was killed in World War II and who has been accused of betraying the French resistance group to which he belonged. As Curry tracks down the surviving members of the network, he falls in love with Jacqueline, his son's former lover, and eventually confronts the double agent who betrayed Bobbie and his comrades to the Germans. Stern based his story of treason on a true account of a spy ring in Jean Overton Fuller's *Double Webs*.[20] In 1981 *In Any Case* was republished by Second Chance Press as *The Chaleur Network*.

Teeth, Dying and Other Matters is a collection of stories written between 1949 and 1962. Also included in the volume are "The Pursuit of Washington," an essay about Stern's unsuccessful attempts in 1959 to interview John Kennedy and Richard Nixon, and "The Gamesman's Island," an unproduced three-act play about an inventor of games and his husband-swapping daughters. Several of the stories are set in Europe. In "The Assessment of an Amateur," for example, a young American in Paris on a Fulbright loses his small interest in the arts as a result of his acquaintance with Dave Higgins, a gifted American pianist and an even more gifted moocher. Other stories in the volume, especially "Teeth," "Wanderers," and "Dying," offer tragicomic renderings of urban loneliness and failed communication.

Stern's next book, the novel *Stitch*, came out of his experience of living in Italy with his family on a Fulbright in 1962-63. It was during this time that Stern made the acquaintance of Ezra Pound, a writer of great importance to Stern. On one of his visits to the aging poet Stern mentioned a comic story he had heard about Pound's life in Paris. With unexpected rancor, Pound accused Stern of fabricating the story. Insulted, hurt, angry, Stern sat silent for a while, then stood to leave. He went to Pound's side to apologize for upsetting him and to say farewell. To Stern's surprise, Pound gripped his hand and apologized.[21] In *Stitch* Pound is transformed into octogenarian sculptor Thaddeus Stitch, who has been given his own island near Venice where he works (less and less frequently) on his masterpiece, a series of connected forms representing the history of Western civilization. Though his best years as an artist are well behind him, Stitch continues to have a powerful impact on those around him, especially the American Edward Gunther, whom Stitch insults when Gunther visits his house for tea.

1968: A Short Novel, An Urban Idyll, Five Stories, and Two Trade Notes was published in 1970.[22] As its title suggests, the book is a gathering of fictions of varying lengths and kinds. The novella *Veni, Vidi . . . Wendt*, first published in the *Paris Review* in 1970, follows the erotic (mis)fortunes of composer Jeffrey Wendt; the work is a satire on American academic life and a portrait of a failed marriage. *1968* also contains "The Idylls of Dugan and Strunk," which traces two University of Chicago fundraisers who with their younger girlfriends topple out of their ivory tower onto riot-torn South 63rd in Chicago on the night of the assassination of Martin Luther King, Jr. The twin ironic stories "Gaps" and "Gifts" are about sexually restless men and their relationships with a daughter in one story and a son in the other. There is also "Storymaking," a fictionalized portrait of Philip Roth not long after the death of Roth's ex-wife and right before the publication of *Portnoy's Complaint*.

With characters like Edward Gunther in *Stitch* (an earlier version of Gunther had appeared in the story "Orvieto Dominoes, Bolsena Eels" in *Teeth*) and Jeffrey Wendt in *Veni, Vidi . . . Wendt*, Stern was gradually but unmistakably beginning to rely on his own experiences as material for his fiction. Though Gunther differed in most respects from his maker (especially Gunther's aimlessness and sloth), his "bad experience" with Stitch paralleled the one Stern had with Pound. The composer Wendt was even closer to self-portraiture. One thing both Gunther and Wendt (and a few other male protagonists in *1968*) have in common is the condition of being unhappily married. The repetition of this theme suggests a personal source.

In the summer of 1969, while teaching a writing course at Harvard, Stern fell in love with one of his students, Alane Rollings, who was during the regular year an undergraduate at Bryn Mawr. Their affair continued beyond the summer; eventually it was discovered, and in 1972, Gay and Richard Stern were divorced. Rollings, who received her B.A. and M.A. from the University of Chicago, became Stern's constant companion and an impressive poet. In 1985, after years of keeping separate apartments, Rollings and Stern married. The story of the affair and the divorce is transmuted into the novel *Other Men's Daughters*, which was published in 1973.[23] Harvard professor of physiology Robert Merriwether meets and falls in love with Swarthmore undergraduate Cynthia Ryder, who is in Cambridge for the summer session. The novel traces with great subtlety and compassion the course of their love affair and its chief consequences, Merriwether's rejuvenation and the painful dissolution of his marriage.

Although primarily a writer of stories and novels, Stern has also published dozens of poems and translations, more than 40 pieces of reportage and criticism, and more than 70 reviews in a variety of newspapers and literary journals. Most of these pieces, as well as excerpts from one of his unproduced plays, "Dossier Earth," are gathered in Stern's three "orderly miscellanies," a genre Stern compares to a "bouillabaisse, the Plaza, and such collections of odd pieces as the *Arabian Nights*, the Greek and Confucian anthologies, the *Mahabarata*, and, God help us, the Bible" (*PB*, x). The first of these miscellanies, *The Books in Fred Hampton's Apartment*, appeared in 1973, a few months before *Other Men's Daughters*. Stern's other two collections, *The Invention of the Real* and *The Position of the Body*, were published in 1982 and 1986, respectively.

In Stern's sixth novel, *Natural Shocks* (1978), well-known journalist Frederick Wursup is asked by a magazine editor to write an essay on death, and reluctantly he agrees.[24] In the process of writing the essay he meets and falls in love with an 18-year-old woman dying of melanoma. The novel offers a grim exploration of journalism, celebrity, friendship, and death in America in the late 1970s. In 1980 Stern published *Packages*, his third collection of stories. Like the first two, this one displays his talent and versatility as a story writer. "Packages" and "Dr. Cahn's Visit" are two very different yet complementary stories about the loss of parents to death and senility (Stern's mother and father died within six months of one another in 1978-79). "Wissler Remembers" offers a gentle revery about teaching, while "Mail" is about a cartographer cum minor poet and his many correspondences. "Riordan's Fiftieth" depicts a Chicago bus driver who maintains his dignity and cheerfulness even though his bitter wife and television-glazed children have forgotten his birthday. Three stories ("A Recital for the Pope," "Troubles," and "The Ideal Address") are written from the point of view of strong, likable female characters.

In 1986 Stern published his seventh novel, *A Father's Words*, which presents Cyrus Riemer's attempt to understand and be understood by his four grown children, especially his eldest son, Jack.[25] An editor of a well regarded scientific newsletter, Riemer is greatly troubled by Jack's unwillingness, despite obvious intelligence and ability, to make anything of his life. What is unique about this classic struggle between father and son is that it is told in the first person from the frustrated, guilty, sorrowful, angry father's point of view. Stern has conceded that *A Father's Words* is another of his autobiographical fictions (*PB*, 180).

In 1989 Grove Press published *Noble Rot: Stories 1949-1988*, which includes all the stories in *Packages* as well as many from *Teeth* and *1968*.[26] In addition, *Noble Rot* offers six previously uncollected stories. One of these, "The Sorrows of Captain Schreiber," became the second chapter of *Europe: Or Up and Down with Baggish and Schreiber*. The other previously uncollected stories are of more recent vintage, though the experimental "Losing Color" uses names of characters in *Stitch*. "In the Dock," originally part of *A Father's Words*, presents Cyrus Riemer's encounter with an incredibly emasculating woman. The two most powerful "new" stories in the volume are "Zhoof" and "La Pourriture Noble." In "Zhoof" a Jewish advertising model named Powdermaker is shocked into new awareness when he is insulted by an anti-Semitic French couple in the dining car of a train riding through the Italian Alps. "La Pourriture Noble," the volume's title story in French, is about Derek Mottram, a retired and somewhat retiring wine salesman, who is visited on Christmas Eve by Denis Sellinbon, the troubled, troublesome son of his former business partner.

Shares and Other Fictions was published in 1992; the center-piece of the book is *Shares: A Novel in Ten Pieces*, a highly compressed narrative about two brothers, Robert and George Share. Robert is a deputy secretary of state who finds it easier to deal with the crises of the world than with Obie and Reg, his politically critical daughter and his aimless son. George Share is a successful shoe merchant in fictional Willsville, a small town in rural Illinois; a college dropout, George has nevertheless made his "Share Complex" the cultural oasis of his community. Unbeknownst to the citizenry of Willsville, George takes a different attractive young woman – "a Share Fellow" – to Europe each summer. When George and Bug Venerdy, this year's young companion, meet Reg in Venice, the plot takes an explosive turn. Also included in the collection are Stern's 1970 novella *Veni, Vidi . . . Wendt* and four previously uncollected stories: "The Illegibility of the World," "The Degradation of Tenderness," "The Anaximander Fragment," and "In a Word, Trowbridge." Relations between parents and their children are important in all but "The Anaximander Fragment" (an ironic story about love and accountability set in Saudi Arabia during Operation Desert Storm). In "The Degradation of Tenderness" Alfred and his outlandish, publicity-seeking girlfriend, Porphyria Ostreiker, bring about the demise of Alfred's psychiatrist father in revenge for the case studies on his daughter and son the father has published in a professional journal. "In a Word, Trowbridge" offers middle-aged daughter Charlotte Trowbridge's long overdue declaration of independence from the insidious influence of her famous artist parents (her father dead, her mother still deadeningly alive).

In 1992 Stern completed a draft of a nonfiction book, *Quickly, Quickly*, a "sistermony" about his relationship with Ruth Stern Leviton, who died of cancer in 1991. He has also assembled a fourth collection of essays – on writers and writing – titled *One Person and Another*.[27] In addition, Stern was at work in 1992 on a new novel about a Hollywood filmmaker named Ezra Keneret; according to

Stern, this may turn out to be his first "modern" work of fiction.[28] Stern continues to do reviews and reportage, including a short piece on Senator Alan Simpson's misappropriation of Shakespeare during the Clarence Thomas hearings. Stern even covered the 1992 Wimbledon tennis tournament for the *Chicago Tribune*.[29] In other words, at 65 in 1993, Stern seems more prolific than ever.

Critical Motifs and Qualifications

Given the length of his career, the variety of his work, and his penchant for going his own way, Richard Stern is not an easy author to classify. Critics, friendly and otherwise, have proffered labels over the years, but few of these labels stick without a lot of qualifying glue. The description of Stern as a "writer's writer," for example, is appropriate in the sense that he is someone who has devoted his life to the study, teaching, and writing of serious literature. The tag is also suitable if it is meant to suggest that he has a strong following among writers, that his work is greatly admired by those best qualified to judge and appreciate artistic achievement.

But "writer's writer" also carries with it connotations of not appealing to a popular audience – or, for that matter, to commercial publishers. And, indeed, Stern's difficulty in staying with a single publisher to some degree bears out this more negative meaning of the term. But this pejorative meaning is unfair if the implication is that his work appeals only to writers. Stern himself has been emphatic on this point: his audience may not be large, he has said, but it is diverse, composed of lawyers, dentists, salespeople, nurses, and stock brokers, as well as poets and novelists and literary scholars. Writing in *Chicago*, John Seelye expresses a similar opinion: "Richard Stern is not . . . a 'writer's writer,' though he has been called that, but he is a reader's writer, which is, one would suppose, the best kind."[30] The tag "writer's writer" may also suggest that Stern's novels and stories are usually about writers. In fact, Stern resolved early in his career not to use writers (at least not creative writers – his fiction does include a few journalists and editors of newsletters of various kinds) as his protagonists. The range of Stern's characters is perhaps best seen in the stories, where it is not uncommon to find among his protagonists a bus driver, a real estate

broker, a travel agent, a wine merchant, a hotel clerk, a diplomat, the
wife of an egotistical graduate student, a cartographer (who, admittedly, is also a part-time poet), two university fundraisers, and a
composer of popular songs.

Like "writer's writer" the description "academic writer" has
been used to describe (and, depending on the critic, to praise or
condemn) Stern. Like "writer's writer," the label has a certain validity: virtually Stern's entire career as an author has coincided with his
job of teaching at the University of Chicago. The effect of this close
association with the academy is apparent in several respects. The
rich range of cultural allusion – to books, architecture, music, and
painting – and the great importance that ideas play in his fictions are
what one would expect of an academic, a genuine intellectual. Furthermore, several of his most memorable stories ("Good Morrow,
Swine," "Teeth," and "Wissler Remembers") and novels (*Other
Men's Daughters*) and the novella *Veni, Vidi . . . Wendt* have teach-
ers as their protagonists. Novelist Douglas Unger, who studied with
Stern at Chicago, has written that "Stern's fiction almost invariably
revolves around the university, or at least the scholarly in vocation."
According to Unger, "the motive behind his novels is as much to
discover relationships of ideas as of relationships of his characters
and their situations. . . . All of Stern's novels choose real subjects,
with their scholars or practitioners as main characters. Nets of ideas,
what Stern has called his 'stuff' or 'matter' – as if facing an impene-
trable mass of it in the creative process – this is what the story and
characters bounce back and forth over and are finally captured
in."[31]

An important aspect for Stern of being an academic has been
that teaching has given him the security to write to please himself
rather than to please a large, commercial audience. "My whole life
has been planned," he said in a 1978 interview, "so that I could
make a living in the university, so that I don't have to live on my
writing" (Birtwistle, 184). At other times, however, Stern has
acknowledged the danger inherent in such security, the temptation
of writing for a coterie, or of taking too much delight in allusiveness
and obliquity. Sometimes he has even told himself that he has taken
the easy way, that perhaps his work would have been better if he
had been forced by necessity to appeal to a broader audience. "I
didn't have the guts," he admits in one interview, "made quickly for

shore, told myself I had to pay the rent, buy the kids shoes" (Atlas). But such moments of self-doubt about his career are rare. Though he admits to occasional bad classes, even bad semesters ("it's like getting kicked in the stomach over and over" [Birtwistle, 186], he says), Stern is someone who genuinely loves teaching and the University of Chicago. He has even defended the academy as a world as worthy to be written about as any other: "In a university one can be lonely; one can cheat, love, be loved; one can be heroic, villainous. One breathes, eats, works, pays, engenders. What the writer writes about – alteration, doubt, illusion, gain, loss, forgiveness – are not these in the university as in every human nutshell? And for those who work with 'the times,' what other twentieth-century institution is at once pulpit, seedbed, laboratory, marketplace, the crossroads of what's been and what's to be?" (*FH*, 163). These observations aside, it is important to recall that not all of Stern's books, and even fewer of his stories, are set in universities, and though virtually all of his protagonists are thinkers, not all of them are professors, or even intellectuals – in his words, "I've also got intelligent people who don't know Cézanne's address" (Atlas).

Stern is also called a "Jewish writer," and here too the fit is less than perfect. As he likes to point out, he is not usually included in the "Hart, Schaffner & Marx . . . haberdashery" of Jewish writers Bellow, Malamud, and Roth (the joke is Bellow's) (*IR*, 221). In a 1961 talk on Jewish writers Stern said that he had become conscious of his "place not as a Jewish writer but as a writer who was also a Jew even though his material had never been explicitly Jewish" (*FH*, 155). When he made this claim, only one of his stories ("The Good European") had a leading character who was specifically a Jew, though after writing *Golk* Stern says that he belatedly realized that Herbert Hondorp, the book's protagonist, and Hondorp's father are clearly Jewish (*FH*, 155). Since 1961 Stern has written several stories that feature Jewish characters, the best being "Wanderers," "Packages," "Dr. Cahn's Visit," and "Zhoof." And more than one of the novels has a protagonist who is identified as a Jew: Edward Gunther in *Stitch*, Jeffrey Wendt in *Veni, Vidi . . . Wendt*, Frederick Wursup in *Natural Shocks*, and Cyrus Riemer in *A Father's Words*. Yet with the exception of "The Good European," "Wanderers," and "Zhoof," and perhaps *Stitch*, Jewishness per se is not an important issue for these characters or for the works in which they appear. In

1978 Stern said that he had yet to write his "Jewish novel" (*IR*, 221), and in 1992 this was still the case.

The Jewish influence, the sensibility, is a different matter. In subtle, indirect ways, it pervades much, perhaps even all, of Stern's fiction. For instance, in his essay "Country Fiddlers, City Slickers: Virtuosi and Realists" Stern observes that many of the leading contemporary American realists are Jews, while the leading "virtuosi" today tend to be gentiles. The reason for this curious division, he speculates, is that

> Most of the Jewish writers I know come from families which were actively melting into the great American pot. The family direction was Americanization, that is, movement toward open-ended prosperity and full acceptance. Newcomers to games usually play by the rules. Is it too much to say that the novel-writing children of these new Americans tended to play by the narrative rules? Their books – filled with an American experience which usually ended in triumph or bittersweet loss – toe, often brilliantly, the realistic narrative line. (*PB*, 50)

Though Stern's schema borders on the simplistic (much of the essay presents exceptions to the rule), his theory has an obvious relevance to his own case. The pressure to assimilate has not only been an important factor in the lives of his parents and grandparents; it has also profoundly affected Stern's practice as a writer. Paradoxically, he is most Jewish – that is, most representative of many assimilated American-Jewish writers – in his avoidance of explicitly "Jewish" themes.

Another label, not unrelated to "Jewish writer," that comes up occasionally in reviews is that Stern is a "comic writer." Many of Stern's stories and novels have humor in them, and the humor takes many forms, from wisecracking dialogue to witty allusion to furious diatribe to gentle self-mockery. Moreover, Stern's works are usually life-affirming. But most often Stern's humor and comic vision arise from a realist's sense of life's limitations, hardships, and sorrows. In some works, like *Natural Shocks*, there is more sorrow than laughter, more gloom than affirmative vision. Some themes, especially the theme of betrayal, are played out in different keys (ranging from comic to tragic) in different works. In other words, Stern is probably more tragicomic than comic. Much of the laughter is through the tears, in the throat of sickness and death. Thus, Doris Grumbach has written, "Richard Stern is American letters' unsung comic writer about serious matters."[32]

There are perhaps even better reasons to call Stern an "autobiographical writer," especially as Stern has conceded that many of his works since the mid- to late 1960s have their origins in experiences from his life. Yet even "autobiographical writer" should be applied to Stern with caution. First of all, Stern makes a serious effort to disguise and transform the real people and situations that inspire his fictions. Once he is engaged in a work of fiction, further-more, esthetic considerations take precedence over his desire to record what actually happened. In "Inside Narcissus," Stern's impor-tant essay on autobiographical fiction, he writes,

> The fiction writer's story, even when it originates in actuality, comes to be dominated not by it as much as by the writer's feeling of coherence, ampli-tude, pace, his preferred ratio of scene to monologue, vertical – or sensuous – horizontal – or narrative – matter, his sense of comic or pathetic form, or what have you. And of course every alteration made to suit such pref-erences entails others. Reportorial omission deforms not just truth but the whole enterprise of reporting; fictional omission is intended to intensify and embellish; it is a requirement of most fiction. (*IR*, 189)

In fact, the desire to transcribe reality has never been a primary motive with Stern.

That most of Stern's fiction since the late sixties springs from the facts of his own life does not mean that readers must know every one (or any) of the correspondences that exists between life and art to understand and appreciate his work. The stories and novels are self-contained. There are no self-conscious references to the author or to writing that disrupt the fictional dream. Of course, those who know Stern have the added pleasure of tracing parallels between his life and art, but such knowledge (Stern would call it gossip) probably hinders more than it enhances esthetic pleasure. The only real justi-fication for mentioning the autobiographical element in Stern's art is that he discusses the issue in essays and interviews. Some of Stern's comments on his autobiographical practice read like contrite confes-sions and promises never to write about his life again; nevertheless, he continues to draw consciously on the materials of his life for his fiction.

Writer's writer, academic writer, Jewish writer, comic (or tragi-comic) writer, autobiographical writer – each of these tags has some merit as a description of Stern, at least for specific works. Yet each also falls short of truly capturing the essential quality of his fiction. Perhaps the difficulty of describing him says more about his art than any label possibly could.

Chapter Two

Stern Style

> For as long as I can remember, I have liked words on a page. . . . I have some
> sense of the way words and sentences and paragraphs relate to each other. A
> good deal of myself seems to get expressed – or at least pleased – by lan-
> guage arrangements.[1]

Praise for Richard Stern's style goes back at least as far as the
responses to his first novel, *Golk* ("a clean, oblique style reminiscent
of Nathanael West . . . loaded with that kind of recognition junkies
call *the flash*," Joan Didion), and readers have sounded such praise
with the publication of each successive book (*Europe* is "made out
of the joy of language, witty and always entertaining, it is a beauti-
fully-contrived artifact," Anthony Burgess; the stories in *Teeth* are
"fine examples of economy, intelligence, and literary tact," Stephen
Donadio; *Stitch* is "a gem of high wit written by a master of the language," Thomas Berger; Stern's prose in *1968* is "as dazzling as early
sunshine in cloudless winter: it makes you blink," *TLS*; *Noble Rot*
presents "some of the liveliest and most eloquent stories in American
fiction," James Marcus; and so on).[2] Yet the word *style* encompasses
so many different things, from small elements like the cadence of
words in a sentence, or sentences in a paragraph, to large ones like
the extended use of juxtaposition and counterpoint in a novel, to
even larger ones like the humaneness, humor, or sanity of a writer's
voice. The style of every Stern story and novel is to some degree different, made to suit the narrative demands of that work. And it is also
true that Stern's style has evolved over time. In the last decade, for
example, his prose has become increasingly fluid and conversational,
especially in *A Father's Words*, in the stories published for the first
time in *Noble Rot*, and in *Shares and Other Fictions*. This change
may well reflect Stern's practice since 1979 of composing his first
drafts by dictation to a student assistant; he has had several different
assistants over the years (*PB*, 177-79).

Realists and Virtuosi

A good place to begin a discussion of Stern's style is with the distinc-
tion between "realists and virtuosi" that he makes in his essay
"Country Fiddlers, City Slickers: Virtuosi and Realists" (*PB*, 44-51).
According to Stern, the "virtuosi" are those writers who descend
from James Joyce and who include contemporaries like John Barth,
Robert Coover (a former Stern student), and the late Donald
Barthelme. A writer of this kind "takes off from other writers' works.
His virtuosity strikes the eye immediately: his language is different,
the arrangement of it is different. We feel the eloquence, farce, fantasy, and technical mastery of his work" (44). For such experimental
writers, the manner of telling a story is usually as important, and
often more important, than the story itself. The realist, on the other
hand, "focuses on what's *there* or could be. The realist wants his
work to seem real" (44). For the realist, style is never an end in itself
but instead serves the ends of the narrative. Stern's distinction is not
unlike the one John Gardner makes in *The Art of Fiction*: Gardner
distinguishes between writers who try to create a "vivid and contin-
uous dream" of reality and writers of "metafiction," for whom the
object is to dispel the narrative illusion of traditional fiction and to
remind the reader of the author's presence.[3]

Since his style has been praised so often, Stern might be
expected to list himself as a virtuoso, or at least to admit that he
aspires to be included in this class of writers. Yet Stern places himself
squarely in the realist camp, though he acknowledges, perhaps
thinking of his own work, that realists can aspire to stylistic elegance,
and also that many realists have "virtuoso impulses" (45). But usually for Stern, the story – the action and characters, especially the
characters – is more important than the manner in which the story is
told. Or, rather, the way the story or novel is told is subordinate to
and inseparable from the action and characters. "For me," Stern
writes in his essay "Underway" (1986), "narrative naïveté is essential, and, at least until revision, stylistic naïveté is essential also. My
energy goes into the construction of a story which seems beautiful
and moving to me. Language is, of course, a powerful component of
the beauty, but I do not engage it immediately as [Yukio] Mishima
claimed Japanese writers engage Japanese and Italo Calvino claimed
Italian writers engage the problems of their dialects and Italian. Nor

do I wish to make such engagement the center of my work" (*PB*, 191). Stern once described a work-in-progress (*Veni, Vidi . . . Wendt*) as being "one that discards most temptations to show itself being written, one that still hews to the standard narrative illusion" (*FH* 142).[4] For Stern, this is the higher – or at least the more valuable – art, not just the art of Saul Bellow but that of Henry James, Ford Madox Ford, Stendhal, Proust, and Chekhov.

Within the ranks of realists, however, Stern makes other divisions. For example, there are the "surface realists," writers whose fiction bears a clear relation to "post-Mondrian – Minimalist – painting, post-Brancusi sculpture, post-Webern music" and ultimately to "the laser and silicon chip" (*PB*, 52). Stern has especially admired the "understated, bare, deceptive, and rather chilly art" of story writers Raymond Carver, Mary Robison, Tobias Wolff, Amy Hempel, Bette Pesetsky, and Ann Beattie, all of them descendents of "Sherwood Anderson and his treacherous disciple, Hemingway" (52-53). But though he can admire their art, it is not enough for him. "My own preference – and practice," he writes, "is for fuller, more richly detailed" fiction (53). (Stern makes his remarks in an essay about short stories, but what he says applies to his taste in novels as well.) According to Stern, the masters of this fuller kind of fiction since World War II include Saul Bellow, John Cheever, Peter Taylor, J. F. Powers, Philip Roth, Bernard Malamud, John Updike, and Flannery O'Connor. Bobbie Ann Mason (of *Shiloh*) and Barry Hannah (of *Airships*) are, in his opinion, more recent masters in this line (53).

The fullness of Stern's stories and novels is one of their most recognizable characteristics – especially their intellectual fullness. References to the great thinkers and artists of Western (and sometimes even Eastern) civilization abound. Thus Frank MacShane writes, "Richard Stern, himself an intellectual, a man for whom music and reading and the plastic arts are as important as, though no more important than, other human experience, includes them in his fiction as easily as less developed writers use fishing or baseball as their frames of reference."[5] Partly, this ease of reference comes from Stern's life in the academy, especially an academy like the University of Chicago. But most American writers of our age have university affiliations; few, if any, cram so many intellectual and cultural allusions into their work.

With characteristic self-deprecation Stern once denied in an
interview that he thinks of himself as a "particularly intelligent person" or even as a "deeply-read person," but he added that he feels
an obligation to "put as much as [he] can handle" into each story
and novel. "Why should one try for less than the best?" he asked
(Anderson, 106-7). In a few instances some readers might wish that
Stern had held back: academic discourses on German history in
Europe: Or Up and Down With Baggish and Schreiber or some of
Stitch's more allusive stream-of-consciousness passages, which run
the danger of being inaccessible even to readers who know something about Ezra Pound and modernism. Such passages make clear
why Stern's novels have not sold in drugstores and supermarkets and
explain why he has sometimes been attacked by reviewers for being
difficult or obscure. In a review of *1968*, for example, D. A. N. Jones
complains that "Stern's English is Butch Academic, allusive and
exclusive, mingling a studied demotic with a little learning, none too
lightly worn, so that each sentence seems designed to impress rather
than communicate."[6] Reactions like Jones's are exceptions (Jones's
being easily the most extreme) rather than the rule, as are Stern's
flights into obscurity. Still, Jones's caricature does point to an important aspect of Stern's style, his delight in allusion and obliquity, his
reluctance to articulate as much for the average reader as he could.[7]

Nor are allusions to art, music, literature, philosophy and history
the only things to be found in Stern's fiction. The author also displays what Philip Roth calls as "enviable and dazzling knowledge of
the globe's daily business."[8] His realist's eye is continually drawn to
the time-bound and the local, be it a meal in an Italian restaurant on
Amsterdam Avenue in New York or the face of a Russian soldier at a
checkpoint in East Berlin. Titles of television shows, brands of men's
clothing, names of popular entertainers, sports figures, and politicians – even the bowel movement of his protagonist before he makes
love in the novel *The Chaleur Network* – these things are as likely to
show up in Stern's fiction as are references to Nietzsche or Monet or
the *Divine Comedy*. Reviewing Stern's short stories, Sven Birkerts
writes that "all have been rendered with a fascination for
circumstance and setting – for the why and how of their
dailiness – and with an eye for their psychological particularity."[9]
Culture-laden and cerebral, on the one hand, bound to the minutiae
of daily life on the other, Stern's style is an unusually rich blend of

the universal and the idiosyncratic, the cerebral and the sensual, the spiritual and the mundane. Stern's voice, writes Bernard Rodgers, Jr., mixes "the street and the library, what he has seen and heard and what he has read and thought."[10]

Stern and Bellow

Rodgers's formulation sounds a lot like a description of Saul Bellow's voice. And the comparison of the two writers is a natural one to make, for they have many things in common in addition to a close friendship. Both, for example, are Jewish, and to some degree both at times seem ambivalent about being Jewish – or at least both at times have a tendency to "seem Jewish and not Jewish" (Atlas). Both live in Chicago and work at the University of Chicago and have done so for decades. Stern, in fact, played a part in recruiting Bellow (Atlas). Both have used Chicago and even the same Hyde Park neighborhood as settings for stories and novels (*Herzog* for Bellow, *A Father's Words* for Stern). Most important, both write about intellectuals, usually men, caught in a tragicomic struggle with the world, with other people (often women), and with themselves.

But there are also important differences between Stern's work and Bellow's, differences that Stern's reviewers have sometimes ignored. After conceding the parallels between Stern and Bellow, Sven Birkerts observes that Bellow wins the Nobel Prize while Stern "gets seen as the shadow-man":

> Such superficial perceptions can play havoc with a worthy writer's reputation, and need to be countered. For Stern is no more derivative of Bellow than, say, Raymond Carver was of Hemingway. These resemblances are nothing beside the differences of style, temperature, and vision. Bellow is a seeker, a metaphysical dramaturge; his focus is on the soul condition of late-20th-century man. Stern is a crisper and quicker talent. He is a realist looking at the here and now. He is Chekhov to the other's Tolstoy, and to choose between them is a mistake. (46)

Typical of the kind of comparisons Birkerts describes is the one in *Kirkus Reviews* on *Noble Rot*: "Like Bellow, Stern peoples his stories with cosmopolitan talkers and bookish dyspeptics. . . . But that says it all – Stern's *like* a lot of other writers, who do what he does, only better."[11] Birkerts may also have had in mind John Bowers's review of *A Father's Words* in the *New York Times Book Review* that unfavorably – and absurdly – contrasts Stern not with Bellow but with Tolstoy: "Tolstoy was a cannoneer. . . . Richard Stern may best be compared to a jeweler."[12]

The frequency with which his work is viewed in relation to Bellow's has obviously been a sore point for Stern, even perhaps when the comparison favors Stern (e.g., Peter Prescott's comment in *Newsweek* that Stern is like Bellow but "without Bellow's viscosity").[13] No writer of stature in America, with the possible exception of Mark Harris, has been a more enthusiastic champion of Bellow's fiction than has Stern (Bellow has in turn been a great admirer of Stern's work). And Stern has declared on more than one occasion that the advantages of being Bellow's friend have far outweighed the disadvantages. Stern credits his friend and colleague with helping him to "aim higher," as well as with offering advice about specific works. For example, one of the best scenes in *Golk*, the office confrontation between Golk and his two epigone betrayers, resulted from a criticism Bellow had made of an earlier draft of the novel (Atlas). Bellow, no doubt, has also profitted from Stern's critiques. At different times in their careers each has been a first reader of the other's manuscripts. Despite such benefits, there is no question that Stern's career has also in some ways suffered from his proximity to his Nobel Prize – winning friend.

The differences between Bellow and Stern, Birkerts shrewdly remarks, are differences finally of intention and genre, and such differences are manifested most clearly in differences of style. Bellow comes to fiction from the study of philosophy and social thought. His is an expansive, a discursive genius. As Stern has said, Bellow has the "desire to comment – often brilliantly – on everything around him" (Appendix). By contrast, Stern comes to fiction as a writer and student of poetry, especially the modern poetry of Eliot and Pound. In describing the end of *The Waste Land* Stern also characterizes many of his own works: "The end of the poem is a collection of fragments, a microcosm of the Pounded poem, that rapid, jagged, elliptical juxtaposition of brilliant scenes and cultural shards which became the flag of modernity" (*FH*, 301). Stern's impulse is not to expand or expound but to allude, contrast, contract, and compress. The

"characteristic tone" of his fiction "as well as its strategy of development," writes Marcus Klein, "is created by ironic modulations."[14]

"From the time I started writing, which was before I was a
teenager," Stern told one interviewer, "I must have been hooked by
concision. The more mileage you got from the shortest expenditure
of energy was the aesthetic principle."[15] A compulsive reviser, Stern
admits to writing more than 40 drafts of some passages. Every sentence, every word must count, must be special. Stern hates "filler
sentences" and "imprecisions." When he goes over a story he sees
"excess stuff" (McQuade, 126). This impulse to compress, this
atomic intensity, has led more than one reviewer to observe that
some of his short stories pack as much material, as much thought
and feeling, as one would expect to find in a novel. And though it is a
source of pleasure for Stern's admirers, this concision is also a
source of Stern's difficulty. "Stern's short stories are short," writes
Mark Harris. "His novels and reportage have always been concise,
compressed. Economy of language is his rule. Because of this economy, I think, he has not been read easily."[16]

The desire to compress has also led Stern to rely heavily on
highly charged figurative language, especially metaphor and simile.
Sometimes, in fact, entire stories and novels are unified by image
clusters. In his autobiographical fictions Stern often creates imagery
that is suggested by the profession of his protagonist or of one of the
other characters. Thus images of thirst and satiety run through *Other
Men's Daughters* where protagonist Robert Merriwether is a dipsol-
ogist. The dominant image pattern in *Natural Shocks* comes from
protagonist Fred Wursup's girlfriend, Sookie Gompert, a geologist.
There are places in the early works where such reliance on figurative
language seems strained. The following passage from *The Chaleur
Network*, though it may be designed to show the pretentiousness of
first-person narrator Samuel Curry, seems stilted and overwritten by
today's standards: "A perfectly civil beginning, almost too civil, for I
felt like someone applying for a visa. There was this thumb of a man
with the huge glass of liquid orange sitting back waiting for me to
pour my appeal out, while I wanted him to be trotting out bandages
and cold compresses for my family wound" (18-19).

Many times in the same novel, however, Stern delights the reader
with images that startle and amaze. Here is the same narrator, a con-
summate sensualist, eating trout in a restaurant: "I had two bites of

the fish, marvelous, clean, toasty, a taste that seemed to come and go like a gull hunting scraps" (97). Such moments of metaphoric power are not reserved just for *The Chaleur Network*; they are generously interspersed throughout the pages of the Stern canon. In his story "Teeth" a frigid Chicago street comes to life: "Out on Fifty-Third Street, the wind was knifed for murder. People passed like thugs, scarves pulled over mouths, hats down like old Dr. Hobbie's to the nose. Ridges of steel ice humped the streets, and every third corner had its famished crocodile of open car hood, whining for life" (*NR*, 66). In "Packages" a son observes his mother in a hospital bed, stricken with cancer: "The last hours, teeth out, face caved in, the wrestler Death twisting the jaw off her face, she managed a smile (a human movement) when I said we were there, we loved her" (*NR*, 366).

Stern would be the first to say that Saul Bellow has done many remarkable things in his stories and novels – things Stern would never even attempt. By the same token, Bellow could not have, and would not have, written the image of the gull hunting scraps. The image belongs to Stern, as do the crocodile car hoods and the wrestler Death. There are many windows in the house of fiction. Bellow's windows are not Stern's. Stern's windows – small, jagged, brightly polished, some clear, some opaque, some reflecting diving gulls – are not Bellow's either. Nor should they be.

Quiet Innovations

Even though Stern does not count himself as one of the practicing virtuosi of post–World War II American fiction, he has been interested in stylistic innovation within the tradition of literary realism since the start of his career, and he has often been singled out for his originality of form and expression. Thus Richard Ellmann wrote of *In Any Case* that "one must read it to find out what the American novel is up to."[17] In a similar vein, a reviewer for the *Manchester Guardian* wrote that Stern is "one of the handful of American writers whose experimentation seems to spring from some really original quality of perception and not just from a craving for novelty."[18]

Stern's interest in pushing the boundaries of the short story goes back at least as far as his student days at the University of Iowa where he says "a few of us were deciding that the James-Lubbock-Brooks-Warren-Tate notion of the perfected story was finished. 'Break the windows, open the doors. Air.' Yet *Augie March* looked too crude for some – 'What a style!' *We* knew it was time to take off Flaubert's corset. And to throw away Joyce's glue, shears, and colored markers" (*IR*, 136). Stern says that as a story writer he learned early how to pack a lot up front – a device that invariably manages to hook readers and keep them turning the pages. In his highly perceptive review of *Noble Rot*, Sven Birkerts elaborates on this technique: "The stories . . . almost always plunge us in medias res and set our reading antennae to bristling. We have to work to sort out the references, chronologies, and twists; half the time the key to a given story is buried in a casual remark or snatch of off-kilter dialogue. While the exertion is initially great, often slowing our involvement, the payoff is worth it" (Birkerts, 47). Later in the same review Birkerts notes Stern's (and Chekhov's) preference for the "diminuendo ending, especially for . . . narratives of ill-sorted love." The burst of action at the beginning and the quiet, often disappointed finish are appropriate to Stern's realist's vision – a vision that sees life itself as an arena in which, Birkerts writes, "the spume of fantasy and expectation" gets played out "against the limiting wall of circumstance and human nature" (48).

More than 80 percent of the stories in *Noble Rot* (and roughly 70 percent of Stern's novels) are written in the third person. Yet this is an almost meaningless statistic since Stern's narrations are so supple and mercurial in their movements from third to second and first person and then back to third. Thus the story "Teeth" begins in the second person before it settles into third:

> Ah, Miss Wilmott, how did you come to think what you did? Is all your inter-preting so askew, so deformed by self-interest? And is your self-interest so unbroken a pup that any street whistle seems its master's voice? To think that you were misled as wisdom itself was being certified in your aching jaws? Those third molars, so long held back, and then so painfully emergent, fangs and cusps clinging savagely to the gum flesh."Impacted," said Dr. Hobbie, and despite the kind, soft-beaked, confident face behind the metal glasses, you shuddered. (*NR*, 60)

The tone here is at once mocking and compassionate as Miss Wilmott, an instructor of history at the University of Chicago, falls

hard for her dentist, Dr. Hobbie. The dental references, the wisdom
teeth puns, perhaps date back to Stern's oral surgeon father, but the
exposure of poor, lonely Miss Wilmott, her soul laid bare, is the work
of a different kind of surgeon.

Stern's ease in shifting from one point of view to another is
matched by his skill at moving back and forth through time. In a
review of *Other Men's Daughters* James R. Frakes praises Stern's
"use of some unusual time-patterns, with convolutions and overlays,
flashbacks and flash forwards."[19] In a 1986 interview Stern com-
mented about the fluidity of point of view and time scheme in his
fiction: "That's one great thing about being a fiction writer: one can
go in and out of consciousness, one can shake up time, one can
switch from exposition to scene, one can do almost anything. It's the
equivalent of sensuous power in the other arts; fiction writers don't
have marble, or sound, or actors. What we do have is fluidity; so
shaking up the time scheme is part of that."[20]

Some of Stern's stories are conventionally plotted. In "Lesson
for the Day," for example, unemployed graduate student Mervyn
Kiest (his incompetent wife has the academic job) sets out to seduce
the wife of pompous divinity student Jimmy Deschay. The story pro-
ceeds more or less chronologically and ends in an unexpected triumph for Kiest when he rescues Deschay, who has gone mute in the
pulpit. It is not the sexual conquest he dreamed of, but it is something, and the story's conclusion suggests Kiest will try again another
day. Other Stern stories like "Mail" and "Wissler Remembers" are
organized by association of memories. There are even a few overtly
experimental efforts. "A Short History of Love" and the manic "Good
Morrow, Swine," both written before 1950, are told almost entirely
in dialogue. "Losing Color," a story about attempted suicide, is as
dreamlike as any of the avant-garde fare published in the littlest of little magazines.

Stern's novels also show a restless range of innovation, though
Stern rarely resorts to gimmickry. In one essay, however, he mentions trying to write "a narrative in which different elements of narra-
tion itself relate the story over or through the author's head. So
'Voice,' 'Plot,' and 'Subject' make their narrative claims." After
"hundreds of pages and hours" on the project Stern published only
four pages as "introductory" at the end of *1968* (*PB*, 47). In *Europe*
he creates a character (Juliette) whose sole purpose is to comment

on the structure of the novel in which she appears. Whenever she faces a blank page, she says to herself,

> " 'Juliette, sweetheart, write me something new, something different, something which displaces this single-situation tyranny . . . , something which knocks the reader on the head by bringing in characters who don't recur, situations which work only in the roundabout ways of contrast and comparison.' I never let the reader take hold. When he thinks he has me, I'm not there. Ha, ha, ha, ha, ha," and she slapped her forehead. (151)

A few lines later Juliette says that she has even introduced into her new novel a "character, an obnoxious one, imported clearly for the purpose," who defends the technique of the book (151). In other words she not only describes the structure of *Europe* but also herself and her role in that novel. Such an excursion into metafiction is extremely rare for Stern. Usually his experiments are quieter, more subtle.

The strategy of withholding narrative closure that Juliette describes, however, is one that Stern employs in several novels. For example, Stern once described his novel *Natural Shocks* as resembling a "Jackson Pollock painting. The book seems a constant agitation, nothing is quite let go. Every time you think a story line will be resolved, it isn't. Something else opens up" (*IR*, 223). In a sense, this refusal to give in to what the reader expects – and sometimes desires – is a strategy in all of Stern's novels. Thus *The Chaleur Network*, Stern's novel about espionage, relentlessly uncovers layer upon layer of deceit, until the narrator and reader are forced to recognize through sheer exhaustion the futility of distinguishing between loyalty and treason, innocence and guilt. Of *Other Men's Daughters* James R. Frakes states that Stern renders his characters "unsentimentally persuasive by . . . uncompromising honesty and unblinking comprehensiveness." And, Frakes adds, "one of the miracles of this novel is how such comprehensiveness is achieved with so much economy, so many ellipses" (Frakes, 5). Stern's novel *Shares* is only 71 pages long (though in earlier versions it was nearly 300). The idea in this work of fiction, Stern explains, is to "suggest character and narrative development without drawing it out."[21] According to the book's jacket, *Shares* is "a work that is neither a short novel (although it's short), a full-length novel (although it has some of the weight, action, and scenery of one), nor a condensed novel (although it uses techniques of condensation." There are brilliant scenes in *Shares*, but no character is present long enough to evoke from the reader the kind of empathy Stern creates for his characters in his longer novels.

In the final analysis, the quality that sets Stern's work apart from that of others is his desire not to say anything in the usual way. Stern has maintained that novelists live or die according to their *novel*ty, their difference from other writers (*FH*, 221). This continual striving for a uniqueness that combines elegance and complexity, comprehensiveness and concision, is evident in every sentence, every paragraph, every story, and every novel that he has written. The accolades of many of his reviewers (despite a D. A. N. Jones or two along the way) testify to that uniqueness. Even the names of his characters, according to Tom Rogers, bear Stern's inimitable stamp: "What distinguishes this Chicagoan from almost every other writer is, first, the names he gives his characters: Holleb, Dochel, Strunk, Kahn, Kiest, Scharf. Stern loves short, dense, dark, mouth-filling, explosive-sounding names, and he writes stories about such people in what might be called a dochel, scharf-like, kiestian prose. 'Dying' begins: *Dreban's first call came while Bly was in the laboratory.* No one else writes that way. Just to pronounce the sentence requires extraordinary and energetic lip and mouth movement."[22]

Stern would no doubt regard Rogers's comment – that "no one else writes that way" – as the highest praise.

Chapter Three

Geniuses and Epigones

"So there they go," said Golk to Fitch, who was packing away a camera behind a flap of the cave. "My successors. The epigones."

"What's that?" asked Fitch. (*Golk*, 182-83)

Richard Stern has always been fascinated by famous people, or at least by those among the famous genuinely worthy of fame. In interviews and autobiographical essays, Stern has recalled with great warmth his childhood chance encounters in New York City with the likes of Sinclair Lewis, pianist Artur Schnabel, and Albert Einstein, as well as with baseball players Red Rolfe and Joe DiMaggio (*IR*, 214; also Atlas; also the Appendix). In adult life Stern has enjoyed a similar proximity to stars – a proximity he has often done much to cultivate. As a writer and as a private citizen, Stern has sought out, observed, and recorded his impressions of a wide range of celebrated people: scientists, philosophers, musicians, artists, politicians, actors, journalists, television newscasters, and, most often, other creative writers. Great inventors, regardless of the form their inventions take, have always called forth Stern's deepest fascination. "My whole life," Stern says, "I have pursued these people. What is the best, the most interesting thing going?" (Appendix). His answers to this question fill scores of journals he has been keeping for several decades. His published portraits of Robert Lowell, Lillian Hellman, Saul Bellow, Philip Roth, Flannery O'Connor, Ezra Pound, and others hint at a buried trove of valuable material yet to be discovered.

What are Stern's motives for seeking out these great inventors? Does he bask in reflected glory, perhaps to soothe an ego wounded by popular neglect? Does he hope to profit in some way, to advance his own career, or if nothing else, drop a famous name or two whenever he wishes? Or does he hope to nurture and inspire the great inventor in himself? Stern would no doubt wonder at this questioning of his motives. He would say that he is fascinated by these people because genius is always fascinating, always a delight and a surprise. "I get assidious about recording some of the things they say," he told Jim Spencer, a reporter for the *Chicago Tribune*. "I feel like I have a kind of obligation to posterity to do that, to let people know what some of these remarkable people said in off hours, what they thought, what they looked like, what their feelings were."[1]

Approaching the Great Inventors

Not surprisingly, the subject of creative genius has also been an important theme in Stern's fiction, especially in two of his early novels, *Golk* and *Stitch*. The title characters of both books are great artists, though the nature of their genius, the arts in which they excel, and the worlds where they invent differ greatly. *Golk*'s setting is New York during the early days of television, while *Stitch* conjures a world of expatriate American artists and writers in Venice in 1962-63. Golk (real name Sydney Pomeroy) is the originator and driving force behind the successful television show "You're on Camera"; the novel in which he figures traces "the sensational bloom and conclusion of his career" (*Golk*, 99). Stitch, on the other hand, is a famous sculptor, but his career as a productive artist ended many years before the start of the novel that bears his name. His chief distinction in his ailing old age is that he was witness to, important catalyst of, and major participant in the modernist movement of the early twentieth century.

Both novels are grounded in real experiences and, in the case of *Stitch*, even real people Stern had encountered. Stern no doubt drew on his days working at Paramount Films International for his depiction of corporate power and greed in *Golk*, especially in its uniquely American concoction of art for huge profits. He also used his early experience as a viewer of television: "new in my life back then and felt as its power is felt in those first weeks. (Like a hick's first day in New York)" ("On *Golk*," 32). The success with which Stern captures this world is measured nicely by Bernard Rodgers, Jr., in his Foreword to the 1987 University of Chicago Press reprint of the novel: "Twenty-seven years after its initial publication, *Golk* remains noteworthy as one of the first – and with [Jerzy] Kosinski's *Being There*, still one of the few – treatments of the character and impact of television in serious American fiction. Its moving and hilarious portrait of Poppa Hondorp, mesmerized in front of the screen; its black comic treatment of the world of ratings battles, midlevel media managers, and godlike network moguls that would later be captured in the film *Network*; its witty demonstration of how this powerful new medium quickly began to create its own language; its exploration of Golk's and Hondorp's Faustian bargains with the medium – all retain their freshness" (viii).

The prototype for Golk was Allen Funt, the originator and star of the television show "Candid Camera." Stern had never met Funt, but he greatly enjoyed "Candid Camera," and before that, Funt's radio show, "Candid Mike," as well as his movie shorts.[2] Like Funt, Golk's most prominent physical trait is his bald head, and throughout the novel that head is described in ways that suggest its connection with Golk's brilliance. Stern also gives Golk two skills that he admired in Funt. The first is the ability to blend into any background. When Herbert Hondorp, the book's protagonist, first meets Golk, for example, the latter is perfectly camouflaged in the window of a fish shop: "Golk seemed part and parcel of the display, a monster specimen who'd disgorged the others. The chameleon knack, the rare trick of being one's environment, this was Golk's most unusual gift as an actor in his own scenes. What one would have sworn was an absolutely uncamouflageable skull had passed over New York as that of a race tout, corporation lawyer, Bombay Yogi, ex-prelim middleweight, lion-tender, pickpocket, Belgian poet, and God knows what else" (18).

Another of Funt's traits that Stern gives to Golk is the ability to spot talented amateurs for his skits, but Golk takes this gift a step further by recruiting many of his victims to become his assistants in "golking" other victims: "Golk's instinct for the misplaced life, the sheared gift, the convertibility of his fellows was like a poet's gift for metaphor, although more single-minded: the direction of the conversion was always the same: the world's victims were transformed into his own and then into the exploiters of other victims" (93).

For all the resemblances to Funt, however, Golk is not meant to be a portrait. Funt is merely a starting point for the fiction. Stern's creation is a master dramatist and psychologist, gifted with almost omniscient powers – his "golks" strip bare the pretentions and absurdities of his victims with epiphanic clarity. Incredibly, most of these victims do not seem to mind being exposed as fools or worse; they readily sign the release that promises them their precious seconds of fame. In all this a resemblance to Funt can be seen, but unlike Funt Stern's great inventor is seized by a "virus of ambition" (166). He is never long satisfied with what he has done; his aspirations lead inevitably to his downfall.

The origin of *Stitch* was Stern's becoming acquainted with Ezra Pound in Venice in 1962-63. Long before he first met Pound the poet was an important figure for Stern – a hero in fact. Pound was one of four writers (Joyce, Eliot, and Proust were the others) who "took up a lot of [his] apprentice time" (*FH*, 283). Stern's second published article (in *Accent* in 1953) was "Pound as Translator," a review essay about Pound's *Spirit of Romance* and *The Translations of Ezra Pound*.[3] In another essay (written in 1967) Stern praises Pound as "a kind of Niels Bohr of the arts, not only a great practitioner but the creator of climates in which other men did their best work" (*FH*, 289-90). Thus Stern credits Pound with creating an "atmospheric receptivity" that "enabled Joyce to attempt far more than he otherwise would have" (*FH*, 287). As for Pound's own work as a poet, Stern asserts that Pound's "quest and practice altered the language and literature of this century" and that *The Cantos* is "the only modern American poem that can approach the *Comedy*, *Faust*, and the classic epics" (*FH*, 289-90). Stern has even been something of an apologist for Pound's war crimes: "in a black period of his life his not wholly misdirected rage at the war-linked cultures of industrial society became a frenzy of imprecision, and it was not difficult to lump him with far more evil men and events" (289).[4]

In *Stitch* Pound is transformed from famous poet to famous sculptor Thaddeus Stitch, and instead of *The Cantos* we have Sant Ilario, the small island ("stranded, antique, a paleolithic city" [*Stitch*, 102]) on which Stitch has labored for decades to complete his magnum opus, a series of connected forms representing the history of Western thought and culture: "Eighty or ninety yards squared from water edge to water edge, five hundred, maybe a thousand colors firing up from blocks, spheres, triangles, polygons, thousands of colored shapes, some surfacing as people, horses, turtles, plants, silos, villas" (37). Like Pound, Stitch has spent 10 years incarcerated in a mental institution in the United States for making radio broadcasts (many of them anti-Semitic) for the fascists during World War II.

Like Pound when Stern knew him in Venice in 1962-63, Stitch is now at the end of his career, tormented by what he has failed to accomplish: "And what he left, his sixty years' work, was so oblique, so dark. When he'd wanted above all ascent into light, enlightenment, order . . . the human order which mirrored the cosmos, the divine ordering. Years and years, what were they now if he'd left only disorder, hints, scattered notes? Waste" (25). Again like the Pound Stern encountered, Stitch fears that he is losing his memory. The powerfully dramatized image of memory loss, in fact, becomes the novel's chief metaphor for the end of transmission, the death of European culture. So like his original is Stitch that the novel has been praised as biography. Poet Karl Shapiro has written that *Stitch* is "the best most decent thing ever written about Pound," a view echoed by Hugh Kenner and others.[5]

In *Golk* and *Stitch* Stern approaches his great inventors indirectly, through lesser figures, followers – "epigones" – who are, technically speaking, the antiheroic protagonists of their respective novels. These characters both reflect and offer a contrast to the title characters; furthermore, their lives are radically transformed as a result of coming into contact with Golk in one book and with Stitch in the other. This technique of approaching the great inventor indirectly is one Stern said he borrowed from *Madame Bovary*, *Anna Karenina*, and *The Sun Also Rises*. "You begin by indirection, with the weak," Stern explains, "and you approach strength through veils."[6]

Herbert Hondorp, the protagonist-reflector of *Golk*, is a 37-year-old ex–poli sci major who has never held a job in his life. Supported by his doting ear-nose-and-throat-doctor father, Hondorp spends his days in "endless, unpressured leisure," wandering through the shops and bookstores of New York (21). His only dread is being asked what he does for a living, and this is exactly what he is asked one day by an unseen voice emanating from a dusty shelf at the back of a second-hand bookstore. The voice, we soon learn, belongs to none other than the great Golk himself, who watches Hondorp on a monitor from across the street in a fish shop. It is a moment Hondorp has long hoped for: to be discovered by Golk and used in one of his skits.

Even better than getting "golked" is the invitation Hondorp receives to help cage the next victim, another customer in the book-

store to whom Hondorp shows a slip of paper that is seemingly covered with Shakespeare's handwriting. Visions of wealth and fame
dancing in his brain, the customer tries to cheat Hondorp and the
bookstore owner, until Golk's hidden voice denounces the man as a
"swindler," an action that sends the startled victim out of the store
and down the street in a "galloping waddle" (17). After Hondorp
performs his role to perfection, Golk invites him to join his crew.
Hondorp protests that he has no skills, but Golk reassures him that
"we'll make your skills for you" (21). The invitation offers Hondorp
the chance to become a participant in life instead of an observer. It
is also Hondorp's chance to end his puerile dependence on his
father – an opportunity he seizes with Oedipal zeal. Ironically, as
Hondorp sheds one father, he gains a new one in his mentor, Golk.

The protagonist-reflector of *Stitch* is 35-year-old Chicagoan
Edward Gunther. Hungry for the intellectual stimulation and cultural
richness of Europe, Gunther has quit his job as an ad man, sold his
house, and pulled his wife, Cressida, and three children with him to
Venice, depleting the family savings in the process, much to Cressida's distress. Gunther's relationship with Stitch, though it changes
during the course of the novel, is quite different from Hondorp's
with Golk. Initially at least, Gunther stands in awe of Stitch. When he
and his family are invited to the great artist's house for tea on
Christmas Day, Gunther regards the occasion as "an investiture of
cultural nobility" (55). Stitch's view of Gunther, unfortunately, is far
less generous; to Stitch, Gunther is a "fathead" who is "dazzled by
celebrity, a groveler" (24). During the tea in Stitch's home, the great
artist is deliberately rude and accuses Gunther of "inventing fifty-
eight per cent of what he says" (60). Edward is devastated by the
experience. When he gets up to leave, he apologizes for upsetting
the old man, only to be surprised once again by Stitch who declares
his life's work a failure and also apologizes in his way: "Wrong,
wrong, wrong. . . . Eighty-seven per cent wrong. I've never been able
to recognize benevolence" (62). In other words, Stitch says to Gunther what Pound had said to Stern.

Golk and *Stitch* are similar in yet another important way: the
protagonists of both novels become romantically involved with
women who are closely connected with the great inventor of each
novel. Hondorp, in fact, gets involved with two women who are part
of Golk's retinue. Elaine, a beautiful "Negress" whose seductive

manner is a deliberate caricature of a white man's dream of black sexuality, relieves Hondorp's initial nervousness on the job with a depleting after-hours session in her bed. Hondorp's more serious liaison is with Jeanine Hendricks, who is assigned by Golk the task of whipping Hondorp into shape. Beautiful, strong, independent, hard-edged, streetwise and embittered, Hendricks is typical of many of the women in Stern's early stories and novels. A devotee of the "cult of experience," she models herself on Stendhal's Lamiel. At 23, she has survived marriage to an English sadist and been rescued by Golk, with whom she has had a brief affair. But for Golk "falling in love seems . . . an almost sure sign of failure" (50).

By the time Hondorp joins the crew Golk has not called Hendricks for sex or companionship for five months. Presumably, this has added to her bitterness toward Golk and men generally. Hendricks at first underestimates Hondorp, and when Golk, disguised as a patient, captures Hondorp's father on film, Hendricks chides her student for giving in to "that kind of shit" (81). Hondorp, however, proves a quick study. When Hendricks later pulls a stunt of her own by leaving Hondorp naked and asleep on a Long Island beach (after making love with him) to be discovered by her grandmother, Hondorp warns her never to use him as a prop again. The episode marks Hondorp's attainment of parity with his teacher; at this moment their alliance is born. Not long after this scene, Henricks and Hondorp, both reflectors of the greater genius of Golk, fly off to Paris for an extravagant romantic weekend.

The woman in Gunther's life (in addition to his wife) in *Stitch* is Nina Callahan, who in some ways resembles Jeanine Hendricks. Like Hendricks, Nina is strong and independent. But she is also softer, more sensitive. Perhaps her chief difference from Hendricks is that Nina is a serious artist, a poet engaged in writing a feminist epic. For years she has led a hand-to-mouth existence in Europe, most recently in Venice, trusting to the goodwill of those richer than herself and to her skill as a quick sketch artist. Nina regards Eros as the greatest danger to her poetic ambitions. In a passage that makes her sound more than a little like Golk, she reflects, "*love*. Always love. The resort of people who have nothing else. The last phase of materialism" (19). Other poets might sing that "the only gain was loss," but that was where Nina "would get off the male train" (21). She had viewed from a distance the effects on talented women of subjugation to the almighty phallus. Despite her resolve, she finds herself yielding (the first time, admittedly, while intoxicated) to the importunate and unhappily married Edward, as well as to her own long-suppressed erotic desires.

Moments of Truth

It is through Nina that Edward first meets Stitch, and it is also through Nina that many of our impressions of Stitch are shaped. Though Nina gets annoyed with Stitch when he bullies Edward (and with Edward for allowing himself to be bullied), she reveres Stitch and yearns for his approval – the approval of someone who is part of the great tradition: "His praise was grafted upon her confidence, and by the time she heard the downstairs door click shut she felt herself become a new person because of it. She had been recognized by someone in the great tradition" (13). Indeed, it is through Nina that we get a hint of the significance of the great inventor's name – Stitch "stitches" the great past with the artistically diminished present: "It was not merely his being an artist. Nor a fellow exile. Nor was it his being a container of precious memories, though the fact that he had known Valéry and Yeats and Blok and Rilke, and their equivalents in building, painting and music, *was* a kind of miracle. As was the fact that he himself belonged to them. With him, the link was something felt even before she'd known who he was" (8-9).

Stitch, for his part, returns Nina's admiration and also tries his best to keep her away from Edward, for he fears "the little *Irische Kind* . . . was getting tangled in the lines of the poor slob and his domestic sty" (100). In an effort to save her from "the lopsided rhino" (97), Stitch asks Nina to sit for him as he does preliminary work on a bust of her head, even though Stitch has no intention of completing the project. Meanwhile, Nina, who has been stuck on her women's epic, is suddenly swept along on a wave of creative energy, as though she were "played by a giant" (151). For four days she writes continuously. When she stops, she decides to show the poem to Stitch. For her, and perhaps also for the novel, it is the moment of truth, out there on Stitch's island:

> He had praised it as a piece, *sui generis*, but he was seeing her now in that
> long run which was the only one that counted – even in the short run. There

was the great matter and manner, or there wasn't. One discovered or one did not. One added or one did not. One sowed and harvested, or consumed other men's work. Makers or servers: this was the division of artists. (156-57)

Stitch tells her that her "fine work is without love," and by that he means "sexual passion. Love from mind to body" (157). Nina is stung, even momentarily infuriated, by the old man's criticism. Ironically, it is sexual passion that she has perceived all along to be the enemy of her aspirations as a poet.

The rising action of *Golk* involves the progression of "You're on Camera" from local to network program. When Hondorp joins the crew the show's success depends on relatively harmless strategies designed to entertain; when the opportunity comes to present the show to a national audience, however, Golk is no longer content with such skits. Instead he aspires to the role of satirist-surgeon who will expose, punish, and reform. Hondorp and Hendricks nervously caution him against the sins of pride and the dangers of overweening ambition, but Golk defends his shift from light comedy to biting attack by explaining, "I want a taste of it, for its own sake first of all, and secondly because in my nose abuse and bad power and dumbness and harsh force itch and smell, and I think that displaying them in our little golks would be a great blow at them. I'm thinking this is the sort of thing we – the medium and us – may have been intended to do" (104). Golk targets a presidential adviser, a union negotiator, and an official in the petroleum section at the State Department; using techniques that anticipate later governmental (and "60 Minutes" – style) sting operations, he exposes his victims' vanity, arrogance, hypocrisy, and corruption.

"You're on Camera" becomes an overnight sensation, and Golk basks in the show's popularity. Not everyone, however, appreciates the latest "golks." Newspaper editorials condemn "You're on Camera" as a serious threat to the right of privacy. Golk's latest victims sue the network for $45 million, and Parisak, the owner of the network, is forced to settle out of court. In the eyes of Parisak and his executive henchman, Lurcher, Golk had crossed the line of acceptability. Despite Golk's "great gifts," laments Parisak, he "cannot trust Golk's ambition or his tact" (158). Golk has to go. Golk had earlier predicted that this would happen once his exposés were aired. He has known all along that the network cannot tolerate the new:

"Alternation of the lukewarm: that's their formula for novelty, their proclamation of service to the industry and the nation" (86). What Golk fails to anticipate is not his dismissal by Parisak but the treason of Hondorp and Hendricks.

The betrayal of Golk by his two closest subordinates is the crux of the novel, the action to which everything before it builds and from which everything after it flows. The motives of both underlings are complex. From the moment Golk shares his plans to target national figures, Hendricks and Hondorp are concerned about what will happen to them if the show is canceled. On the other hand, both are ambitious, though they (especially Hondorp) glibly condemn this fault in Golk. For Hendricks there is also, perhaps, the added motive of revenge against Golk for abandoning her (as a lover), or, just as likely, for saving her (after her disastrous marriage). As a devotee of "the cult of experience," she does it also for the sheer thrill of doing it, for the "exultant feeling of further liberation from sentimentality" she hopes the treasonous act will bring (172-73). Hondorp's motive is primarily that of ambition, but there is as well an element of Oedipal aggression in his unseating of his mentor, just as there had earlier been this element in the unfeeling way he breaks from his loving, ridiculous father.

Golk's discovery that he has been supplanted occurs in stages. At first he senses an uncharacteristic orderliness in the office, a sensation that leads him to call Elaine to enjoy the comforts of her erotic talents. The next day, however, he notices "the same sluggishness, the same disquieting neatness in the office" (161). This perception leads him to Lurcher's office, where Lurcher downs four fingers' of Haig and Haig scotch and then tells Golk they are not going to renew his contract, that Hendricks and Hondorp will take over, and that Golk is welcome to stay on as "a grand old man of ideas" – an offer everyone knows Golk will refuse (163). Golk's immediate response is to vomit on Lurcher's rug. Then comes the confrontation between Golk and his two underlings. Inspired by "pure hatred," he lures Hendricks and Hondorp into his cave of an office and then into a name-calling contest that culminates in what appears to be Golk's attempt to kill himself by swallowing a yellow pill. Hondorp moans, "Poppa, poppa" (181), while Hendricks sticks her finger in Golk's throat to bring up the pill. Just when they believe that he is dead, however, Golk rises from the floor and announces, "You're on Camera, kiddies," as indeed they are. After Hendricks and Hondorp have departed "like sheets on a laundry line," Golk calls them "epigones," and Fitch asks what that means. Golk explains, "The water after you've washed your socks and underwear in it for a week. Stick with them, Fitch. You'll get no more money from me" (182-83).

Implicit in Golk's label of "epigone" is the failure of "You're on Camera" once he leaves the show. Hendricks and Hondorp get an apartment together (the "wedding party" ends in an epic food fight instigated by Golk), and for a year they enjoy all the trappings of fame and prosperity. But as Hondorp finally acknowledges, they are in it merely "for the damn shekels" (195); whatever small successes the show enjoys are the result of "riffling Golk's files" (192). It is only a matter of time before Parisak and Lurcher cancel the show; in less time the marriage (though never official) between Hendricks and Hondorp collapses. Hondorp moves to Chicago and becomes a deejay, while Hendricks apparently returns to Europe and her cruel first husband. While on a trip to Los Angeles Hondorp visits Paramount studios and sees Golk, metamorphosed yet again, this time into a scene shifter: "Hondorp was just about to shout up at him, when, with a portion of that mysterious insight which always cowed the golks, he looked down, saw Hondorp, smiled, and waved his palm to the right, almost losing his grip on one of the ropes" (206-7). Hondorp returns the salute, leaves the studio, and that night returns to Chicago. Hondorp had once felt himself to be "a Genghis Khan of life come late but fully into his own" (153), but he ends the novel with "all trace of his ambition, all desire for change gone absolutely and for ever" (207).

Stitch's effect on his epigones is more subtle than Golk's on Hendricks and Hondorp, but hardly less powerful. First of all, he plays a role in keeping Nina from Edward when he fixes her up with Edward's cousin, the scholar Wally Sloterman (eventually Nina and Wally become engaged). Nina has grown from her relationship with Stitch. She is honored by his attentions to her, and she becomes stronger by surviving – and rejecting – his criticism of her poem. Although Nina recognizes Stitch's faults, she is able to forgive them. "One thing I guess both of us shouldn't forget," she tells Edward, "is that he's an old man. Older than eighty-year-olds who haven't gone through what he has. We should just take the honor and pleasure of his presence and forget about unraveling what he says" (170).

Stitch has an even more profound effect on Edward. At first glance that effect might seem to be merely negative. Certainly, the beginning of Edward's suffering begins in Stitch's bedroom when the old man insults him. It is a blow to Edward's ego and vanity from which he never completely recovers. And Edward's suffering continues as both his marriage and his very brief affair with Nina disintegrate. By the end of the novel he is unhappy and alone in California, watching John F. Kennedy's funeral on television and pleading on the phone with his wife in Chicago to take him back. She refuses. In the opinion of some readers, Gunther's deflation is richly deserved.

Hugh Kenner, for example, has written that Stern's originality in *Stitch* is to contrast the old sculptor with Edward Gunther. Both men fail, but Gunther, he contends, "fails without style," and that is a crucial difference in a novel that is finally "about the meaning of style" (Kenner, 177). Kenner states that Stitch grows in stature as Edward Gunther diminishes: "And the strength of the book is simply this: that despite an almost overwhelming fictional tradition to which he conforms exactly – he's even Jewish – Edward doesn't amass picaresque *virtu* but dwindles, dwindles. . . . [B]efore our eyes Edward shrinks from the human norm to the International Standard Centimeter, while Stitch comes to incarnate what there is to take heart by" (178-79). Finally, Kenner argues, it is Stitch's "dedication to getting something right, out there on the island," that impresses us, for Stitch embodies those values that must survive if we are to avoid "a civilization of Edward Gunthers" (179).

While Kenner is certainly right about Stitch's artistic integrity, he is too harsh on Gunther. He fails to acknowledge that Gunther's criticism of Stitch and his work has validity. Furthermore, Kenner does not seem to recognize Gunther's considerable capacity to learn and grow and change. This capacity, generated by Stitch's harsh treatment, is his best quality. The shaft Stitch sinks in him takes time to hit its mark, but the pain leads finally to self-awareness, which in turn leads to a desire to transcend his self-absorption: "Couldn't he lose himself in what counted, what belonged to him, what was his human duty to assist and care for? Yes, but first he had to understand what he was. A rusty, backfiring, clotted ego couldn't serve. Clean out the heart" (183). In his introduction to the Arbor House edition of *Stitch*, Frank MacShane agrees with Kenner that Edward begins as "an absurd person," "besotted . . . with himself," "sentimental," totally lacking "the clarity that Stitch has attained, for the little good it did him." But, he adds, Stern does not leave Edward in Venice. Instead we follow Edward back to the states, where he gains a new vision of reality. "We don't know whether he will be saved or whether such a condition is even possible," MacShane states, "but there is change, and that is something" (x).

Art and Politics

The differences between *Golk* and *Stitch* are those one might expect between a first and a fourth novel. The style of the later book is more assured, the characters less schematized according to theme. Although both books explore the phenomenon of the great inventor, Golk invents in the popular medium of television, while Stitch is an artist of high seriousness in the great tradition. The distance between the books, in other words, can be measured by the artistic distance between the two prototypes, Allen Funt and Ezra Pound. Despite these differences, the similarities in technique, structure, and theme are significant. Both novels are built on the contrast between a great inventor and his followers, his epigones. In each book Stern approaches the genius through these lesser figures. In *Golk* the epigones betray their mentor, and in doing so illustrate the gap between them. In *Stitch* the genius figure deliberately, even cruelly, destroys Gunther's sense of himself as well as his affair with Nina. Gunther is singed by his brush with genius; the experience transforms him, but that transformation is in some ways a positive one.

Another important resemblance between Golk and Stitch is that they are overreachers. Both bring trouble, perhaps even ruin, to themselves when their art pursues political rather than purely esthetic ends. Once Golk's motives shift from the desire to entertain to the desire to reform, he makes his greatest impact, but soon enough he loses his forum. Though he is rationalizing his betrayal of his mentor, Hondorp puts his finger on a truth that applies to Golk, and perhaps also to Stitch, when he describes the "virus of ambition which so often attacks men of spirit: it consists in their dissatisfaction with what they do best, because the very ease of accomplishment makes it seem a toy to them, illusion, make-believe. They yearn for the charisma of politicians whose hands can bring a city to tears or

riot" (166). Stitch's foray into politics ended years before the start of
the novel, but the shadow of his activities during World War II, and
of his 3,000 days incarcerated in a mental institution after the war,
throws a gloom over his character and indeed over the entire novel.

Of Pound's war crimes Stern has written that "if Benedict Arnold
had written *War and Peace*, his name wouldn't be a curse; the der-
ilections of Dante and Sir Francis Bacon are shadow depths in our
perspective of them" (*FH*, 289). This is not to say that Stern approves
of Pound's political ideas. Just the opposite is the case. In *Stitch*
Stern's misgivings about Pound's/Stitch's mixture of art and politics
are expressed through Gunther. For example, Gunther objects to
Nina's defense of the generalizing tendency of Stitch's art. He tells
her that artists like Stitch – Utopians and Platonists, those for whom
abstractions count more than individuals – are "bundling singularity
away," "stuffing particulars into ovens," and "violating life." Artists,
Gunther adds, "must be more human, not less. And human is failing"
(112-13). Nina, however, accuses Gunther of "overprizing" singularity. She is bored with psychology and motive and most of the things
that make the sort of art about which Gunther (and the sort of novels about which Stern) cares most (113).

Responding to a symposium question, Stern has written that "the
artist is most political, most social, and most moral when he is being
true to those insights and feelings which in themselves are apolitical,
asocial, and amoral. He deepens and subtilizes human possibility
which counters hatred and anxiety, broadens tolerance, and
reemphasizes the human need for equality" (*PB*, 162-63). Stern's
willingness to forgive Pound's fascism is actually of a piece with his
impatience with those who demand that art be political. In both
cases one can discern a desire to separate politics from art. Art organized to serve didactic political ends is usually bad art and maybe
bad politics too, Stern's comments seem to imply. This is not to say
that Stern has no political ideas or allegiances – he does have them,
has always had them – only that they are not what drives or orga-
nizes his art.

But what of the argument that all utterances, even fictions that
never express a political idea or manifestos that repudiate political
themes in art, are political? What of the argument that those who
take an esthetic, apolitical stance – or even a liberal, pluralistic
approach that seeks to understand and forgive what is human or fal-

lible in all parties and positions – merely support the status quo? Can any writer claim for his or her work the privilege of being above or beyond or unrelated to the problems of the world: war and peace, poverty and hunger, justice and injustice? What have such questions to do with Richard Stern, or with his theme of geniuses and epigones?

Such questions are provoked by *Golk* and *Stitch* and comments Stern has made. The answers, if there can be answers, must be deferred to later discussions in – and outside – this book.

Chapter Four

Americans in Europe

"Best to be an American and live in Europe." (*Stitch*, 59)

Of contemporary American realist writers, few are as skilled at con-juring places as Richard Stern. A restless traveler who has toured six continents, he is unusually responsive to the chaotic shouts of busy city streets, the tastes of bouillabaisse and Gorgonzola, the unex-pected rise of a cathedral arch, footprints and flora and litter on an abandoned beach. Stern packs authenticating details into his narra-tives to give each one a local habitation and a name. Among the familar settings for him, of course, are New York and Chicago, the two cities where he has lived longest and which he knows best. In his stories he brings to life with a few deft brushstrokes the lobbies of New York hotels (filled with "wandering Jews") and the rioting streets of a slum in southside Chicago. Of his novels, *Golk* and *Natural Shocks* take place mainly in New York, while *A Father's Words* is set in Chicago (with a few important scenes in New York). *Veni, Vidi . . . Wendt* unfolds in Santa Barbara, though it ends with composer Wendt and his family back home in Chicago. Most of *Other Men's Daughters* occurs in Cambridge, Massachusetts.

Of all the places that Stern has visited and lived in and written about, however, none seems as important or is used by him as fre-quently as Europe. Roughly one-third of his stories have a European setting, and of the novels only *A Father's Words* and *Veni, Vidi . . . Wendt* fail to take the reader there. In *Golk* Hendricks and Hondorp cement their conspiratorial romance by spending a weekend in Paris. *Europe: Or Up and Down with Baggish and Schreiber* romps through France (Versailles and Paris) and Germany (Heidelberg) before ending quietly in Venice. *The Chaleur Network* is set in France (there are a few recollections of visits to the States as well as a trip to Germany), where protagonist Samuel Curry has lived as an

American expatriate for more than 30 years. Venice, the setting for *Stitch*, is also in a sense that book's protagonist. The adulterous lovers of *Other Men's Daughters* spend a summer in a beautiful villa outside Nice – a place where their relationship ripens into something beyond infatuation. In *Natural Shocks* journalist Fred Wursup travels to Rome to write a story about his friend Tom Doyle – a story that is intended to salvage Doyle's chance for a nomination to run for the U.S. Senate. Later Wursup flies to Bruges. *Shares* has its landscape split between a small town in Illinois, Washington, D.C., and Venice (it ends, however, on the South Pacific island of Moorea).

Hidden Beauties

Obviously, this preoccupation with Europe – especially in the books up to and including *Stitch* in 1965 – is grounded in Stern's own experiences in France and Germany in the late forties and early fifties after he completed his master's degree at Harvard, and in Italy in 1962-63, the year he had a Fulbright to teach in Rome and Venice. And since the early sixties, Stern has continued to visit and enjoy Europe almost every year, especially France and Italy. Even before his first crossing on the *Queen Mary* in 1949, however, Europe was a place of tremendous significance to Stern. First of all, it was the home of his forebears, the place whose hard conditions his grandparents escaped from but toward which they nostalgically yearned. Though as Jews they left behind the life of second-class citizens in Europe, they also brought with them across the Atlantic the conviction that European culture was superior to American culture. The American melting pot was a refuge from persecution and poverty, but American egalitarianism also meant a troubling lack of distinctions, standards, and hierarchy.

This notion of the superiority of things European was also fueled in Stern's case by his study of literature. His favorite authors were either French writers like Stendhal, Flaubert, and Proust or else Americans who lived in European self-exile, particularly Henry James and, with some reservations, the modernist poets T. S. Eliot and Ezra Pound, as well as "Lost Generation" novelists like F. Scott Fitzgerald and Ernest Hemingway.

With the notable exception of Thaddeus Stitch (a version of Pound), Nina Callahan, and a few others, most of Stern's American characters do not cross the ocean to settle permanently. "Europe is usually an interlude in American lives, a pleasure wedged into routine," remarks Samuel Curry of *The Chaleur Network* (90). Curry is another exception; however, he objects to being labeled an "expatriate" because the term is usually "applied to those who found their country uninviting and who went through the world cashing in on their superiority to it" (90). France, he says, is his Chicago, the place where he found work and started a family after World War I. As for the pleasures of Europe that attract Stern's other American characters, they vary from country to country, but each place has its appeal, even post–World War II Germany: "With the sauerbraten, *Figaro*," says Curry. "People will say it was fine to be an American in occupied Germany. Sweet and bitter, bitterly sweet, sauce and music" (125).

In Stern's imaginary landscapes, Europe invariably represents the good life, a nearly infinite variety of delights: the best foods and wines, the most elegant women and most handsome men, the best fashions, architecture, art, literature, history, culture, intellectual stimulation and beauty of every kind. "The place has hidden beauties," says Edward Gunther in *Stitch*. "It's why I came," responds Nina (16). They are talking about Venice, but the delight and discovery could occur just about anywhere from Normandy to Naples, Berlin to the Côte d'Azur.

This absorption in the unique pleasures of Europe is not just a feature of the early stories and novels. Again and again through Stern's fictions characters escape to Europe as a way of sampling the good life. In *Shares*, for instance, George Share is taken by his friend Betsy to a Venetian bakery in the Calle degli Fabri to see "the girl behind the counter, one of those beauties that look as if they have fallen out of a Renaissance canvas onto Venetian streets":

> a Veronese girl, her colors red and gold. The redness had oven heat in it, the gold was pocked with carbon. A working girl, with marvelous solid arms and powerful wrists, her white uniform sported workstains at armpit, breast and belly; her hands were rough, the fingernails short; her nose was blunt, the eyes dark with green glints, her complexion extraordinary, something off a mosaic. Dark gold hair looped in chains around her head.

> What, she asked, did the *signore* desire? George Share could not speak, could hardly breathe. The bakery, full of hot bread smell, dizzied him. He inhaled as if the warm smell rose from the girl's pudenda. Finally he managed to point to a spiral roll. "*Questo*." (*Shares*, 157-58)[1]

The sensual mix of the culinary and the carnal, of gold and carbon, of the girl's stained armpits and the canvases of Renaissance art, creates a wonderfully rich (but hardly atypical) Sternian moment for his American characters as they partake of the great feast.

Europe is also a place to have experiences, to learn about life, about oneself. Theodore Baggish, in fact, cites the Emersonian notion that Americans go to Europe to get Americanized. As a teenager Jeanine Hendricks, the independent female lead in *Golk*, "went through Europe assiduously, almost studiously, appraising her experience and discarding it after appraisal" (*Golk*, 46). It is her idea to fly with Hondorp to Paris for the weekend, perhaps with the motive of initiating him into the world's best college of life. Hondorp is almost overwhelmed by what he sees and feels: "Today, riding up the Rue de Rivoli to the hotel, he felt that he was in the most self-conscious place in the world, a place that demanded that you become conscious of it, of its unlikeness to any place that you'd been, a place that demanded that your life be shaped by, in, or against it. 'The real thing,' Hondorp thought as he put down the pen. 'No golk. The real thing. I'm here'" (152). Hendricks's response to Paris is more exuberant than her pupil's: "Her appetite for experience was revived by what left Hondorp hanging from his fears, the pursuit of novelty for its own sake, and she faced France like a college junior" (151).

In addition to learning, there is also freedom, especially freedom from puritanical American restraint, especially sexual restraint. From the first stories and novels to the most recent, Stern's Europe is a sexual playground, and the liaisons his mostly male characters enjoy are too numerous to list. One reason that Baggish first travels to France "was that he shared the American folklore view that one sort of experience was most readily acquired there" (*Europe*, 43), and that experience was of women. In some of Stern's works, the relation between the sexually hungry Americans and their Euro-paramours resembles that of plunderer to plundered, rapist to raped. In "Gaps" middle-aged travel agent William McCoshan picks up Christine, a young hitchhiker on the French Riviera. After he asks her to pose "before a wall on which was scrawled in charcoal, '*U.S. Assassins. Viet Cong vaincra*'" (*NR*, 55), they find a beach and swim. In the water McCoshan catches her ankle and asks if she surrenders (56). When they make love in the sand, McCoshan realizes the girl is a virgin. The political parallels are impossible to ignore: sexual plunder becomes a metaphor for plunder of other kinds. Not all the sexual relations are exploitative; there are occasions, especially with Max Schreiber in his intercourse with Traudis, when the American is the one taken for a ride. Even when both sexual partners are American (as they are in the early story "A Short History of Love," as well as in the relationship between Gunther and Nina in *Stitch*), the continental climate seems to loosen resistance.

Though sexual freedom is an important lure for Stern's characters, it is not the only kind of freedom they find there. Nina Callahan tells Gunther that it is easier for a woman to live on her own in Europe. It is also perhaps an easier environment for her as an artist (*Stitch*, 18). Gunther, though he delights in the sexual freedoms Europe offers, also relishes the freedom from work. "You have a built-in occupation as a tourist," he says (18). Europe is even the land of opportunity, at least for the rogue hero of *Europe*, Theodore Baggish, who traces the etymology of "Europe" to the phrase "wide prospect"; the notion pleases him, for he knows that "the coastline of his own future was congruent with Europe's, and he scouted both like a bird of prey" (*Europe*, 43). Baggish's rise in Europe, to some degree at Schreiber's expense, is a wonderful exercise in cunning deception and raw opportunism. As one reviewer puts it, "The graph of [Baggish's] ascent from rags in America to riches in the family of a German industrialist, the neat opposite of the historical pattern, is traced with splendid irony."[2] *Shares* has a character whose financial exploits in Europe are reminiscent of Baggish's; Reg Share makes – but unlike Baggish then loses – a small fortune flying hot-air balloons over Venice.

Transmission

Most of Stern's Americans in Europe, however, lack the inclination and the entrepreneurial skills to cash in on their time abroad. Most of their profits are pleasures derived from being in Europe, their pleasures usually converted to profits by and for their European hosts. Unlike Baggish, they cross the Atlantic not just as pleasure seekers but as tourists, Baedekers in hand, anxious to visit the cultural shrines, to immerse themselves in the art, the architecture, the music, the philosophy, the literature, THE TRADITION. Edward Gunther, the protagonist of *Stitch* as well as of two short stories, is the prototype. "A believer in nothing, Edward was still a lover of churches," explains the narrator in "Orvieto Dominos, Bolsena Eels" (*NR*, 283). In *Stitch* Edward tells Nina he is in Europe because of what is there: "The main thing. I wanted to be around what has lasted" (18-19).

These things – churches, great art, the thought and values of past ages – are all the more precious, of course, because they are now imperiled, the great cultural heritage in danger of being forgotten. This is Stitch's great theme, that of the character and of the book that bears his name. As part of the great modernist intellectual wave that broke against the shore of the early twentieth century, Stitch is both endangered species and endangered rememberer. "It's the end of Europe," he thinks to himself in one monologue. "My stuff won't even bubble down. As if it matters. Though it does matter. If there are no survivors, no rememberers" (*Stitch*, 50). Later he says to Gunther, " 'This,' the eyes blinked green, in, out, 'doesn't exist. No Europe any more. The idea of Europe's gone. The last rememberer, crawling out of the wreckage. And I can't. No bonds – the past,' and the voice stopped on the trembling lips" (62). Since he has just insulted Gunther a moment before, it is possible that Stitch is offering his version of an apology, or at least an explanation, for his rudeness. Apology or not, the fear of oblivion (and not just personal oblivion, but the end of everything in our culture that most matters to Stitch) is genuine.

Stitch's point is brought home even more forcefully to Gunther at the end of the novel when, separated from his family, he visits Venice, California. The contrast with the real thing in Europe disturbs him:

the street, the exhausted, green loggia whose cement pillars gushed into identical, cretinous heads. Past filthy, dollar-a-night hostels and stores whose windows were paper rages of discounts, sales, last weeks-in-business, Edward walked. Business. The deadest deadbeat area he'd ever seen. The deadbeats' faces were as dead as the cement ones, their clothes like bandages

on their bleeding lives. Above them, the parodies of Venice, blunted trilobe
windows, an inchoate Ca' d'Oro, a desert-colored Palazzo Ducale with
four cement lions on its corners. (*Stitch*, 198)

On another day, the day of John F. Kennedy's assassination, Edward
stares out his window in amazement at a group of teenage surfers,
for whom "nothing had changed" and never would as long as the
water was there, the sun out, and the tide in. "Their memory,"
Edward realizes, "was yesterday's waves. Reality was what was in
your sights. The past was what you desired right now. Was it what
Stitch was getting at, what made him so gloomy? The present didn't
exist because it was its own past. Was this what he meant by the
death of Europe? The death of transmission? Of memory?" (200).

The concern with the loss of the European tradition has continued to be one of Stern's great themes, both as a writer and as a
teacher. Each year, he writes in one short essay, the gap seems to
widen. His cousin sets up an interview with "one of Hollywood's
most literate agents."[3] Stern begins to tell him about *Stitch*. The
agent stops him when Stern mentions Ezra Pound. "Who's Ezra
Pound?" the agent asks. A television newscaster, a beautiful woman
who would soon be a household name for taking the place of
another household name on a morning news show (only to get supplanted by another beautiful, soon-to-be household name), goes
blank when Stern makes a casual allusion to Jane Austen. His students at the University of Chicago seem each year to know less and
less of Joyce and Proust and Rimbaud, the Bauhaus, or even "of
Vietnam, of Twain and James." Most even read a lot but "are late
starters and show less ability to distinguish excellence from trash"
(*Bostonia*, 9-10). Some of this griping, Stern knows, "is the standard
complaint of age," and at times Stern can sound like cultural conser-
vatives E. D. Hirsch or University of Chicago colleague Allan Bloom.
But Stern lacks the political agenda of either critic. Unlike them,
Stern can appreciate the humor and subtlety of a Jacques Derrida.[4]
He knows more than a little about contemporary African fiction and
poetry, as well as what is hot on the literary scene in South America
and Australia. And if you ask Stern what the best thing going today in
the world of letters is, he does not hesitate to say poetry by women.[5]

But these ways that Stern is "with it," his efforts to remain a contemporary, do not change his sadness about what is being lost, pos-

sibly forever. And that sadness is heightened, sweetened, transmuted by those frequent trips to, and even more frequent thoughts of, Europe.

Hidden Sorrows

Despite the stark contrast between Europe and America offered at the end of *Stitch*, Stern's attitude toward the old country is more ambivalent than simple Europhilia. Or, at least, he is able to parody his own Europhilia, to show that even the love of culture, when carried to extremes, has its destructive side. Thus in *Stitch* Cressida Gunther reflects on the European transformation of her husband, Edward: "Europe had brought out the worst in him, culture-hunting, church-licking, you'd think he was on the verge of conversion to see him eating up the Madonnas, lecturing the kids on their inadequate grasp of Europe's greatness, then exhibiting a behavior that had about as much to do with civilization and culture as a tiger vomiting the remains of a jackal. Adultery, negligence, sloth – despite his typing – waste, getting fat again, his exercise going by the boards. Not that she cared. Let him swell up as big as San Marco" (174). Even Edward concedes in a rare moment of self-reflection that he has been "hogging Italy against the imagined winter of his life. . . . Stuffing for a feast no one would ever eat" (183).

The imagery of gluttony also figures prominently in the story "Orvieto Dominos, Bolsena Eels," which features a slightly altered (i.e., younger, unmarried) Edward Gunther. Keyed to Dante's *Purgatorio*, Canto XXIV (the one depicting Cornice VI: the Gluttonous), the story begins with Edward speeding up the Via Cassia at 90 kilometers an hour with Vicky, a beautiful American woman he has managed to pry loose from her tour group. Before the sexual feast Edward anticipates that evening, they do some sightseeing at a Renaissance château and then a Gothic church in Viterbo, and then the Duomo with Maitani's facade and Signorelli's frescoes in Orvieto. As they are leaving the chapel, however, Vicky is spotted and reclaimed by her tour group. The nearly despairing Edward consoles himself with a huge meal consisting of "a mezzo-liter of Orvieto, pasta, eggplant parmegiano, and roast beef Bolognese" (*NR*, 287). Then he heaves himself up for a walk down the Piazza and another visit to the Duomo.

The next morning Edward stops at a trattoria and eats "six rolls, with butter and jam, and [drinks] two cups of *caffelatte*." He recalls a tercet from Canto XXIV that he had written down for Vicky – "Ebbe la santa Chiesa in le sue braccia; / Dal Torso fu: e purga per digiuno / L'anguille di Bolsena e la vernaccia" – which Gunther translates as "Martin of Tours, who had the Holy Church in his arms, and now, in Purgatory, did without his beloved Bolsena eels cooked in white wine" (*NR*, 290-91). Moments later Edward swims in Lake Bolsena until, that is, he doubles over with cramps and vomits into the lake: "He kicked, slowly, moved his arms, slowly, and slowly, his insides rancid, walking, hopping, swimming, his body emptied of pastry, rolls, the rotted gluttony of the day, he made toward the little beach" (*NR*, 291). His regurgitation in the lake is an apt conclusion to this story of sexual, cultural, and culinary overindulgence.

Edward's love of European art, architecture, and history may be genuine, but it is hardly disinterested. No mere lover of art for art's sake, he is able to make sexual hay of his mastery of Baedecker and other cultural guides. It is the exceptional moment in "Orvieto Dominos, Bolsena Eels," in fact, when he becomes so absorbed by the Signorelli that "he even forgot about Vicky, who, though very happy in the lovely chapel and particularly taken with the sweet, strong blues in Fra Angelico's sections, was getting neck-weary. She sat next to Edward, who, after a minute of not noticing her, put a hand on her knee and said it was wonderful, wasn't it, to which she assented" (*NR*, 286).

Edward Gunther is just one of several male characters in Stern who assume the role of teacher and cultural guide in order to seduce young American women traveling in Europe. Perhaps the most egregious instance of such exploitation occurs with 55-year-old George Share in *Shares*. Share clandestinely takes a different young woman from his small home town in Illinois to Europe each summer. In exchange for the free ride and the cultural lessons, the young women are expected to share George's bed. When he takes 20-year-old Bug Venerdy to Venice, however, the place sours on him, even though for 20 years "Venice has been one of his pick-me-ups" (*Shares*, 143). In part, Share suffers from the exceptional heat, but he is also tired of the "bums, thieves, con men, frauds, every kind of poseur and viper" in this "beautiful, watery zoo" (*Shares*, 143). George becomes so weary of the place and the sexual tactic that depends on the place that he eventually pushes Bug and his nephew Reg together.

Not every Stern character wishes to devour or exploit Europe. Some would be content to understand it, especially its darker side. If his grandparents and parents had instilled in Stern the idea of Europe's cultural superiority, they had also no doubt warned of its class snobbery and anti-Semitism and pogroms. And when he went to Germany in 1950, he knew as much as any American civilian about the death camps. If Stern feels that Ezra Pound wrote some of the greatest verse in English in this century, he knows also that Pound was a fascist who made radio broadcasts for Mussolini. In several stories and novels Stern tries to come to terms with such contradictions in Europe and in himself as a Europhile. In "The Good European" Henry (formerly Heinz) Pfeiffer, a German Jew who had emigrated to America to escape the Nazis, gets the chance to return to Europe when Weber, his American boss in Paris, has a nervous breakdown (Weber suffers from paranoia about all things European). Although initially reluctant to return, Pfeiffer soon rediscovers the pleasures of life in Europe. He even visits the town of his childhood home in Germany, although the home is no longer there. "He had come back home," the narrator says, "and what counted was still there. His country's misery was a version of his own; he saw in her looseness and silly posturing the awkward attempts to atone for the misery she had madly inflicted in her fifteen-year exile from European sanity" (*NR*, 86-87). Pfeiffer's next three weeks in Paris with his wife are "the happiest of their lives." Unfortunately, Weber has a complete recovery, and Pfeiffer is called back to New York. Pfeiffer later wonders if he should have stayed, "and a little later he even wondered whether he had meant 'stayed in Europe' or 'America'" (*NR*, 87).

Arthur Powdermaker, the Jewish photographer's model and protagonist of "Zhoof," does not so much seek to understand or forgive European madness and villainy (at least at the start of the story) as to ignore it. Actually, he makes no effort to ignore; he just fails to think of the bitter past. When he visits Nuremberg, for example, "he thought only of Wagner and Dürer" (*NR*, 298). Then, an incident

occurs on a train riding through the Italian Alps. As he sits at a table
in the dining car, a French couple across the aisle gets up and
departs. Powdermaker overhears the husband say "Zhoof," and
moments later the photographer's model understands the word was
"*jouf*," a "harsh, pejorative version of *juif*" (*NR*, 301). The incident
takes him completely by surprise:

> Sitting with his cold white wine by the beautiful lake, Powdermaker felt as if
> his head had been sliced like a grapefruit and put on a plate. Everything
> cold in the universe poured into his decapitated trunk. His heart thumped, his
> hands shook the wineglass, perspiration rolled from forehead and cheeks to
> the white tablecloth. He felt himself flushing, paling, felt what he almost never
> felt, pure rage. (*NR*, 301)

Powdermaker's anger eventually settles into self-scrutiny and finally
into self-acceptance and forgiveness.

    Europe's Max Schreiber is a much earlier Stern character whose
experience abroad is disillusioning, but Schreiber's disillusionment is
not followed by new awareness. During Schreiber's first stay in
Europe, he falls in love (despite his already being married) with
Micheline, a French girl he meets while serving as an army captain in
Versailles. After a brief affair with Schreiber, she runs off with his
black army driver Tiberius. Back in Europe after the war, newly
divorced from his American wife, Schreiber falls in love with Traudis
Bretzka, a German woman who rooms in the same boardinghouse in
Heidelberg where he has taken residence. After Traudis and
Schreiber spend a romantic evening – they make love outdoors in
the amphitheater of the Philosophenweg and then drink and dispute
for hours with two of Traudis's university friends, Schreiber feels "a
strength surging into his blood which he realized was the rejuvenation he'd hoped would come from his return to Europe" (*Europe*,
87). His hopes for the good life, however, are soon disappointed.
The next day Traudis appears in his doorway to "borrow" 40 marks
for her rent. Schreiber is pained by the experience and even moves
out of the boardinghouse; later, however (thanks to Baggish),
Schreiber and Traudis do get back together.

    Schreiber is a very empathetic person. He even understands
Traudis's Nazi past. As a girl she had loved Hitler with all her heart,
had even been a squad leader for the Madchengruppe. All this
Schreiber understands and forgives: "In Traudis, Schreiber saw the

corruption of a people's spirit by madness and tyrannical villainy, the collapse of lives, of families, of life's sweetness. From this sympathy, his love for her grew, and with it the desire to repair, to salve, to rebuild" (*Europe*, 175). When they travel to Beirut, unfortunately, Traudis runs off with Tiberius, who has in the interim become a millionaire by transporting Middle Eastern oil. Once again depressed, Schreiber agrees to take a job as an emcee in a Beirut nightclub.

The novel ends with Schreiber sailing into Venice, but since he has just accepted his new job in Beirut he has "the odd sensation that he wasn't returning to Europe but leaving it" (*Europe*, 213). And despite his bad amatory experiences there, he is very sorry to leave. Perhaps he realizes that one cannot escape one's character by crossing an ocean. Perhaps he understands that his bad luck with women would probably have happened anywhere. Europe at least has taught him to take each day as it comes (*Europe*, 212). And despite the sorrows, it has given him his best memories.

Whatever the reasons, Schreiber whispers, "So long, dear heart. So long, dear, dear heart" (*Europe*, 213). He speaks for almost all of Stern's Americans in Europe who cannot live there always.

Chapter Five

The Comedy of Failure

I tried to defend myself. "I can't be wrong about everything."
To that her response was, "Wrong again, Cy." ("In the Dock," *NR*, 195)

Hondorp in *Golk*, Schreiber in *Europe*, Gunther in *Stitch* – these are not the only Stern protagonists to end in isolation, disillusionment, and failure. Stern has always been attracted to losers, to characters life has kicked in the stomach, again and again and again. Sometimes other characters kick them too; sometimes they kick themselves. In his early novels even Stern's "strong" characters, geniuses like Golk and Stitch, are notable as much for their overreaching failures as for their successes. This emphasis on failure is if anything more pronounced in Stern's short stories. "Somehow that's a more human and precious thing – failure – than success," Stern has said. "It's more representative of the human condition. Everybody fails. And success is only brief' (McQuade, 128). Whether there is an autobiographical ingredient in this theme is difficult to determine. At first glance, Stern seems very different from most of the bungling burghers and lumpen grotesques who populate his short fiction. Perhaps, however, Stern's lack of great popular success, despite the expectations raised by the enthusiastic critical reception of *Golk* in 1960, has humbled him, softened his pride, made him more sympathetic toward those who suffer the slings and arrows of outrageous fortune.

Because Stern is a realist, many of his stories are about disappointed expectations and diminishing horizons. Lonely souls become more lonely. Contests are entered and lost. Characters who live in the misery of ignorance get enlightened and discover the greater misery of truth. Usually the tone in such stories is compassionate, although traces of detached irony and laughter can almost always be detected as well. The bittersweet mingling of humor and sadness is one of Stern's special gifts. The comic and the pathetic in his stories feed each other, turn into each other with unexpected suddenness. In describing William Faulkner's art, Stern also describes his own:

> Faulkner must be thought of as one of the world's great comic writers, great in the sense that his comedy is not finished off with joke, anecdote, or peculiarity, but by pathos and tragedy. There are comic scenes in Faulkner which, written from a slightly different point of view, would not stir a breath of laughter, and there are, as well, immensely moving scenes which could become occasions for roars. Much of Faulkner is border-line, and can be read one way one time, one way another. (*IR*, 58)

Of course the Stern canon contains many purely humorous lines of dialogue, paragraphs of description, and even complete stories, but the humor invariably has its roots in the cruelty of life.

Loners and Losers

Many of the unfortunates in Stern's short stories are losers in love. One of the funniest, and most pathetic, is Miss Ethel Wilmott in "Teeth." A "low-grade instructor" in history "at a high-grade university" (*NR*, 67), Miss Wilmott leads a life of quiet desperation: "her timid six feet, popped eyes and no-nose face – she'd overheard someone say she looked as if she'd been blotted – were no powerful magnet for men" (63). Fortunately she is a genuine scholar – someone who loves research and can even enjoy the freedom to pursue her studies that solitude confers. But not even Miss Wilmott can work all the time. She has spent "hundreds and hundreds of self-pitying hours in her two rooms, Jack Parr jabbering maniacally on the twelve-inch screen while she shared him with *Middlemarch*, its pages stained with the peanut butter she sometimes supposed was more faithful to her than any person on earth" (63). When an abscessed tooth lands her in the chair of Dr. Hobbie, she loses not just her wisdom tooth but her heart. Hobbie is no run-of-the-mill dentist but "a dental genius," an inexpensive one too, who talks about his personal problems as he works on his patients' teeth. His main problem is his wife, Suzanne, "an expert dancer," who regularly manages to get money out of him even though she left him a few months earlier to live with the Bank Building florist, Mr. Consolo (62).

Hobbie does little to encourage Miss Wilmott's romantic yearn-
ings; in fact, he seems unaware of them. He tries to fix her up with
another of his patients, Mr. Givens, a kindly black house
painter/autodidact who fancies himself a Marxist ("the Manifester
and the Working Day being his favorite books of all time" [65]).
Hobbie himself goes dancing each Tuesday until three in the morning at the Tall Boys' Club. At the end of the story Miss Wilmott's
tribulations reach a crisis point. She discovers that her essay on
opium use in nineteenth-century England is based on a serious miscalculation of the number of pounds in a picul. That is not her only
miscalculation. When she suffers from a second abscess she calls
Hobbie in the middle of the night. The good doctor – "this gentle
fool, this *beau sabreur de la bouche*" (73) – picks her up in his car
and takes her to his office. Miss Wilmott is so overjoyed and hopeful
that her pain almost disappears. But after he lances her abscess and
pulls "a bloody three-pronged crown" (74), Hobbie tells Miss
Wilmott that Suzanne and he are back together again, Suzanne being
drawn to return by the money Hobbie inherited when his father
died. As Miss Wilmott sits in Hobbie's car, crying (the dentist thinks
from the trauma of the operation), he tells her that she will be all
right. The narrator, however, quickly cancels such optimism: "She
was not going to be O.K. The Ndembu's troubles left them when
their teeth were pulled; not hers. The Ndembu danced to celebrate;
Dr. Hobbie had not taught her the twist" (75).

At least Miss Wilmott has her research, gets to share a nice din-
ner she made with Mr. Givens, and can look forward to the prospect
of his asking her out some day. She even had a marriage proposal
once, though her suitor was mainly interested in meeting "the scholarly Big Chiefs at Chicago" (63). Worse off is Miss Swindleman, the
cashier at the Hotel Winthrop in New York in "Wanderers." Originally from Synod, Missouri, Miss Swindleman sees her mission in life
as the assimilation of the Jews who live in the hotel and travel to all
parts of the globe, sending her postcards that she keeps on six
boards behind her in her iron cage. She hopes to bring order to
their "avaricious disorder," to teach them the rules (*NR*, 38). Her
postcard collection is her demonstration of that order: "Stability and
place were there amidst the wild shuffling, amidst the packed suit-
cases, the scarred trunks, the taxis to Pier 40" (38). Then there are
the Jews in the hotel who do not like to travel. Mean-spirited Harvey

Mendel, a designer of men's suits, likes to sit in the lobby all day, as much a slave to routine as Miss Swindleman, though Miss Swindleman objects to his fixity, his "cheapness and third-rate vanity" and his "two nut sons" (41).

One day Mendel's business partner, Charley Lepidus, asks Miss Swindleman to give him change for a fifty. When she refuses, because he is not a guest at the hotel, Lepidus storms off to Mendel's room. Not long after this incident, she learns that Lepidus is dead, having fallen out a window – apparently pushed out by Mendel. In recounting how the "accident" occurred, Mendel tells the police that Lepidus returned to his room riled by Miss Swindleman's refusal to change his bill. Lepidus had called Miss Swindleman a "piss-cold anti-*semitischer* virgin-whore" (44) and then started in first on the hotel, next on Mendel. Mendel took the verbal abuse for a while (Lepidus, he says, was "a Hitler with his mouth") but then "caught fire and gave him a push" (45). At the crucial moment Miss Swindleman defends Mendel's character to the detective investigating the death. "An opening had been made," the narrator states. "What does one do about an opening? Send a post card of the Empire State Building to oneself? Go to Mendel's room and say, 'Mendel. I saved you. Now save me. I'm yours. Be mine'?" (46). Instead she does nothing: "The opening was a wound in Miss Swindleman. Days passed, and embarrassment at defending Mendel was all she could stuff in to stop the raw ache. She was altered, but alteration had nowhere to go" (46). The last lines of the story are just as desolate. Six months have passed; Mendel is dead, and Miss Swindleman throws out her postcard collection (which, in fact, is the action that begins the story).

Not all the lonely grotesques in Stern's fiction are protagonists, or women (in fact, only a handful are female). In "Dying" a young instructor in plant physiology at the University of Chicago, Leon Bly, is encouraged by F. Dorfman Dreban to enter a contest to write an epigraph for Dreban's dying mother's tombstone. Bly, whose specialty is senescence, is also an amateur poet who has published a poem in *Harper's* ("theme: 'Oh death, thy sting is life'" [*NR*, 140]), which is how Dreban discovered him. Despite the loyal son's requests by phone that Bly submit a poem, Bly is reluctant, his interests centering mainly on one of his students, Miss Phyllis Gammon. Dreban is persistent (earlier he had tried, unsuccessfully, to entice

submissions from Carl Sandburg and Robert Frost); he even raises
the first prize from $200 to $250. But it is not until Dreban visits Bly
while the latter is playing badminton with Miss Gammon on a hot
Sunday in June that Bly determines to write the poem. Dreban is
dressed in a houndstooth winter overcoat: "In the Renoir blaze of
yard, he was a funereal smear" (146). Despite his wise-guy confidence, Bly fails to win the competition. He gets honorable mention
instead; second prize goes to Mrs. Reiser, a friend of Dreban's
mother – there were three entrants in all. Bly consoles himself in the
arms of Miss Gammon.

Stern often uses this strategy of pairing a relatively normal protagonist with an oddball. In "La Pourriture Noble" retired wine merchant Derek Mottram looks forward to a quiet Christmas alone, his
first in 20 years, sipping Irish whiskey and reading from a stack of
newly acquired paperbacks. But his cherished solitude is broken
when Denis Sellinbon, the son of his former business partner,
appears at Mottram's doorstep, fresh from the Lotus Foot Ashram in
Missouri. It is Denis's third visit to Mottram in the last seven years:
"On a planet of five billion, somehow he, Mottram, had the privilege
of being *the friends* of this pathetic gilk" (*NR*, 343). Denis travels
from ashram to ashram; apparently he is asked to leave each one. He
is also writing a book with the modest title *The World's Mind*, which
he lends to Mottram. The handwritten book is as strange as its creator, spanning from the beginning of time to the present, more a
"listory" than a history, thinks Mottram (356). The pre-Paleolithic
gets one sentence, the life of Philippe de Rothschild four pages.
Denis hopes it will be "a useful guide for schoolchildren, and high
school students can use it to prepare for the SATs" (356).

When Mottram takes Denis with him to a fancy Kenwood man-
sion for a Christmas party, disaster ensues. Denis climbs and soon
ruins $10,000 worth of drapery and refuses to come down until Mot-
tram climbs a ladder to retrieve him; both fall to the carpet below,
Denis on top of poor Mottram. After a brief stay in a psychiatric
ward, Denis returns to Mottram's apartment, much to his host's dis-
may. The next morning, however, Denis has gone off to "Brother
Bull's Lamasery, near Oconomowoc, Wisc" (356). He has taken his
manuscript with him, has Scotch-taped his own ugly watercolor over
Mottram's expensive de Kooning–like nude (Denis takes seriously
the biblical injunction against graven images), and has placed the

ficus tree, a gift from Mottram's daughter, Deirdre, outside on the porch to be killed by frost. "Trees should be left outside," he had told Mottram when he first arrived (342). "I'll never forgive that bastard," vows Mottram (357), but by the end of the story he does forgive him.

Perhaps the most desolate, yet still in some respects comic, of the stories is "East, West . . . Midwest," which also takes place at Christmastime. Protagonist Bidwell, stricken with Hong Kong flu, is a translator, historian, and journalist who is "woefully incomplete and woefully ignorant of it" (*NR*, 88). His hangups, we learn, are "the classic hangups of the twentieth-century burgher" (90), yet these pale before the hangups of Miss Freddy Cameron, whom Bidwell hires to type his translation of the *Secret History of the Mongols*. Miss Cameron disappears with his manuscript for over a week. When he finally tracks her down at her home and retrieves his pages, there are hundreds of mistakes. On Christmas afternoon he receives a call from her; she accuses him of standing naked at her window, of having his way with her. Upset, Bidwell consults a psychologist friend who reassures him that the poor woman is "having an episode" and that she "won't hurt anyone. And she won't throw herself out the window" (94-95).

When Miss Cameron calls again Bidwell agrees to meet with her for coffee at the Illinois Central station in Chicago's Loop. It soon becomes apparent to him that she believes he is Ghengis Kahn ("Chinghis-Kahn," according to historian Bidwell), that she is the warrior's beloved Börte, and that in her womb is their Mongol son. Bidwell tries to persuade her that she has confused the manuscript she is typing with reality, but before he can stop her she runs out of the station.

Four years and a lengthy institutional stay later, she calls again, asking to meet with him. Bidwell reluctantly agrees. She seems to be in better shape than before, perhaps still a little shaky, but calmer, more lucid (she tells him she has given up drinking; Bidwell had not known she had a drinking problem). They arrange to speak on the phone every Thursday and to meet once a month for tea and conversation. When she fails to call after their fourth meeting, Bidwell waits uncomfortably and worries for a while, then persuades himself that "she was out of town, sick, at a movie, or, true revival, she'd faced down her madness, seen through the old delusion" (100). Bidwell should have listened to his fears. The next day's *Sun-Times* reports that Miss Cameron has jumped out a window on the tenth floor of the Playboy Building. Bidwell is "very upset" for a time, then stops thinking of her until the next Thursday, "when the silence of the telephone stirred him." He pities the "death the poor narrow thing had constructed for herself. No campaign, no successor, no trip to the cool mountains, only an elevator ride, a smashed window, an untelephoned farewell: 'This is it. I can't ask you anymore. Let alone by phone' " (101).

Miss Wilmott, Miss Swindleman, F. Dorfman Dreban, Denis Sellinbon, and Miss Cameron do not exhaust Stern's gallery of lonely grotesques, but they do illustrate his ability to portray the sadness, absurdity, and moving beauty of life.

Rare Triumphs

Not every Stern character is a loser, and not every Stern loser is a loser all the time. One way that Stern varies his comedy of diminishing horizons and dying dreams is to throw in the occasional triumph. This strategy of contrast is the structural principle behind *Europe: Or Up and Down with Baggish and Schreiber*, as that book's title suggests. Schreiber's various misfortunes are counterpointed throughout the novel by Baggish's conniving successes. When Schreiber first arrives in Heidelberg, for example, his landlord, Stempel, charges the naive American an extra 40 marks under the table. Later, after Schreiber has left the boardinghouse, Baggish moves into Schreiber's old room. Stempel tries the same rent trick on Baggish, but Baggish refuses to pay the extra 40 marks, despite the dishonest landlord's threats and fury. A similar contrast is afforded by the relationship Schreiber and Baggish have with Traudis Bretzka. She breaks Schreiber's heart on two occasions, but Baggish is only too happy to get the "Traudis-burden . . . off his shoulders" (169).

By juxtaposing the fates of the two characters, Stern adds a poignancy to Schreiber's demise. He also suggests two unattractive alternatives: to be a sympathetic loser like Schreiber or to be an unscrupulous winner like Baggish. This contrast is heightened at those points in the novel where Baggish's rise depends on his successful exploitation of Schreiber's weaknesses. Early in their relationship Baggish sees Schreiber as the means to his end of European prosperity. Schreiber has "an air about him, which, for Baggish, cried, 'Use me. Dupe me.' Without malice aforethought, though without charity, Baggish moved in" (117). Schreiber is so easily used, and so completely blind to Baggish's true nature, that even Baggish feels a tinge of pity for him, though only after Baggish has finished using him. When Schreiber praises his young friend for not being an opportunist like so many young people, Baggish thinks, "Poor dumb jerk . . . . What kind of crud can a man flop around in?" (166).

Baggish's calculated string of triumphs is a rarity among Stern's creations. The more typical pattern is the loser who falls into unexpected, and usually short-lived, good fortune. Stern seems to take a special delight in such stories of sudden success, radical reversals in fortune that transform his characters from slugs to earth shakers. Two such instances in Stern's novels are Hondorp's overnight success in *Golk* and Cyrus Riemer's sudden riches in *A Father's Words*. One year after Golk leaves "You're on Camera" Hondorp and Hendricks are still living luxuriously in their apartment on Sutton Place, enjoying sherry-soaked crabmeat, *petits pois* (served in a silver dish), glasses of Pouilly, and (for Hondorp) splendid Cuban cigars. Hondorp's study is as extravagant as the meals he and Hendricks consume. It houses "three ten-foot walls of books . . . a lounge, a Queen Anne desk with Florentine fittings, and a twenty-eight-inch television set controlled from any of the four armchairs by a switchboard built into the arms just beside pads and pencils" (*Golk*, 197). The remote-control gadgetry would have impressed the novel's 1960 audience; the point of all the luxury, however, is that it will soon be lost by Hondorp and Hendricks forever when they lose the show. No amount of material comfort can compensate for the loss of Golk's creative genius; when it becomes the motive for art, such comfort actually becomes an obstacle to creative success.

The comedy of sudden wealth is milder in *A Father's Words*. When his parents die within eight weeks of one another, Cyrus Riemer inherits a lot of money, enough to change his life and the way he thinks. Much of the new income gets handled, and eventually lost, by congenial stockbroker Billy Jugiello of the firm of Cockroft and Venim. The new money that initially brings so much joy becomes in a short while just another source of anguish for Riemer: "It got so that if stocks were up, then so was I. When they were down, it was gloom-and-doomsville. Six months after mother's death, the market went into a tailspin. I panicked. I got out my charts and saw I was thirty thousand dollars poorer than I'd been a week ago. Even when I hadn't known how I'd pay the next printer's bill I wasn't so panicked" (96-97). So quickly in Stern's fictions do bright things come to confusion.

Cy's shiftless son Jack also has a reversal of fortune when at the end of the novel he creates what promises to be a successful new television series. He flies his father to New York from Chicago to see a pilot episode and later takes him for a meal at Lutèce. Jack, who earlier in the novel lived on peanut butter and Wonder Bread in an unfurnished apartment, orders a $100 bottle of Monbazaillac and boasts that in a couple of years he will make more money than Cy. Cy quietly hopes his son is right, but he has his doubts.

The most dramatic flash in the pan in Stern's fiction is Reg Share in *Shares*. Like Jack in *A Father's Words*, Reg has moved well into his thirties without gainful employment, crippled by Oedipal rage and resentment.[1] In Venice, however, he comes up with the idea of organizing hot air balloon rides over the city. The enterprise is an overnight sensation: his balloons are "featured in newspapers and magazines around the world. His long, clever face was better-known than his father's" (*Shares*, 174). But Reg's fame turns to ignominy when a bomb explodes on one of the flights, killing four people, including the psychotic "friend" who brought the bomb on board. Furthermore, Reg's fall into disgrace and ruin eventually undermines his father's high position at the State Department.

Success for Stern's characters, especially the men, is often measured in units of amatory conquest. An early version of this theme comes in the 1956 story "A Counterfactual Proposition." Freddy Patchell is a philosophy instructor at a small New England woman's college. His dissertation is unfinished; his hours outside the classroom are spent in masturbatory reveries of his days in Europe, a place to which he longs to return for the young women he found there. Patchell's gloomy, "static condition, his internal limpness" (*Teeth*, 59) at the college is roused to some degree by the beautiful but narcissistic student Twyla K. Digges whom Patchell follows around for a year and a half until she becomes his "disease and mania" (61). Relief from his suffering is surprisingly easy. When Twyla arrives on campus one fall semester Patchell is there to carry her bags up to her room. When they get there he takes off a shoe to discard some gravel, and one thing leads to another. Ten minutes into their lovemaking the locked door opens, and Twyla's roommate, Doris, two other young women, and the house mother, Mrs. Pitcher, enter. Caught in flagrante delicto, Patchell seems destined to lose his job when he meets with the college president, Miss Emory, who charges him with moral turpitude. But in this pre–women's liberation male fantasy Patchell is able to enjoy the fruits of his crime. By threatening a lawsuit and bad publicity for the college he wangles a year's research grant at the Bibliothèque Nationale and a letter from Miss Emory to Twyla's father "persuading him to agree to her fervent desire to spend a year at the Sorbonne" (67). Aside from Baggish, no protagonist in Stern is quite as roguish or as successful.

Edward Gunther, the protagonist of *Stitch*, "Orvieto Dominos and Bolsena Eels," and "Recital for the Pope," is always on the make and seems to confirm the theory of characters like Golk and Nina Callahan that love is for those who cannot succeed at anything else.[2] Our sense of Edward as a failure allows us to cheer on his conquests of Nina in *Stitch*, especially the second seduction (the first time she is drunk): "Like a mountain over her, he bore down, brought his thick deer-brown arms around her. The red cape crushed into cloth waves, his dark head under the blocked green felt coming down like a storm on her, while she met his lips, the green brim crumpling, falling off, and their faces rubbing against each other, sucking each other, feeling the sealy muscle of each other's tongue, groaning, fighting for breath. Oh, what discourse. What a symposium" (114). Edward's joys are predictably temporary. While he and Nina race hand in hand through the streets of Venice, making a quick stop at a pharmacy, and then "into Nina's calle" (114), they are spotted by Edward's wife, Cressida. At least Edward enjoys a few hours of pleasure before he returns home and learns that his infidelity has been discovered.

The relationship between stalled career and amorous – most often adulterous – pursuits is also illustrated in *Other Men's Daughters* and *Veni, Vidi . . . Wendt*. In *Other Men's Daughters* Sarah Merriwether, enraged by her middle-aged husband's affair with a Harvard summer-school student, wonders what "profound indolence took hold of him" and prevented him from being a truly "top rank" scientist (139). Clearly she sees his adultery as a compensation for this failure. The link between professional stagnation and libido is even clearer, and certainly more humorously rendered, with Stern's randy composer Jeffrey Wendt. When Patricia Davidov, the sex-starved wife of the Music Department chairman at U.C. Santa Barbara, is late for their rendezvous in the Safeway parking lot, Wendt, his need "large," calls her home and gets into a nasty exchange of insults with her husband. Wendt confesses to the reader that "there's another element" that has fed his manic lust and aggression (*Shares*, 103).[3] Earlier that day he discovered in the *New York Times* that he had not been invited to sign "a big We're for McCarthy Ad," even though "half the lousy composers of New York" are included (103). Patricia never shows for a final farewell tryst. The only satisfaction Wendt can get is shouting abuse on the phone at Patricia's loathsome husband: "Tell your wife to zip your prick to her arse, I have had it with her, I wouldn't touch a cunt you touched with a revolver" (103-4). Venting such anger soothes a wounded ego. Neither sex nor verbal assault equals the joy of a Pulitzer or even perhaps the thrill of inclusion in a "We're for McCarthy" ad, but Stern's beleaguered losers take what they can get.

Mervyn Kiest, the hero of "Lesson for the Day," finds his great moment not in the adulterous bed of Angela Deschay, which is where he would like it to be, but rather in the pulpit rescuing Angela's minister husband, Jimmy, from humiliation. Kiest is an unemployed Ph.D. in English at the University of Wisconsin, his dissertation a study of "the great and terrible John Wilmot, Earl of Rochester" (*NR*, 232). His wife, Dottie, has a soaring academic career, even though she is "a specialist in metrics who couldn't find an accent with a Saint Bernard" (239). "It was," muses Kiest, "WE – Woman's Era – in the universities" (231). Angela Deschay, Dottie's colleague in the English Department, is also a beneficiary of Equal Opportunity Boards, but Angela happens to be a fine scholar and much more, at least in Kiest's opinion. He and Angela walk their children by the lake in Madison and discuss "the seventeenth century, university politics and, after a few awkward skirmishes, sex and marriage" (234).

Kiest is certain that Angela burns for him: "She was the right age, the hot late twenties, and she'd seen around, through, and over her hefty, dull divine" (235). When "dull divine" husband Jimmy gets his first opportunity to preach, the Kiests go with him and Angela to a

church outside Madison. But Jimmy's ministerial debut is a near disaster; after citing the lesson for the day, Matthew 26:23, the power of
words deserts him, and the poor black-robed fool stands mute. Kiest
comes to the rescue. He joins Jimmy in the pulpit, apologizes for his
friend's silence (he tells the congregation Jimmy rose from his sick
bed against his doctor's orders), and then reads the prepared sermon, adding a few choice quotes from the salacious Rochester. Later
that evening Angela calls to express her gratitude. Kiest, who has
spilled his "generative sap" many times on his Sears sheets in
Angela's honor (235), wants her to thank him in person. Angela says
"papers" by way of excuse and then says good-bye (238-39). Kiest
must content himself with his ecclesiastical heroism and a fractured
recital from Dottie of "Frost at Midnight."

Success and failure – these are, of course, relative terms. By
most standards Cyrus Riemer, the protagonist of *A Father's Words*
and the short story "In the Dock," should be able to feel good about
himself. His scientific newsletter has a small circulation but is highly
respected. Cy has a gift for making difficult scientific theories accessible to laymen. In the story "In the Dock," however, he is confronted by the latest girlfriend of his tennis partner, Seldon Dochel.
Seldon's "Nail of the Month" (*NR*, 191), Sylvia, is not just a lawyer;
she is a one-woman demolition squad. When Seldon introduces her
to Cy at the Café Procope in Chicago, she goes right to work (Cy tries
to prevent the inevitable by dominating the discussion for as long as
he can – but to no avail).

First she wants to know why Cy "buries his talent" (199); when
Cy protests that she overestimates his talent, the assault continues:
"Perhaps it's time for you to do something else with your life. I think
you're wasting your talent. You're doing what you're doing because
of inertia. Or sloth. And for peanuts. Is your name in the papers?
Never. I have to ask myself what's going on. What's with Cy Riemer?"
(200). She tells him he is a lucky man because she has "certainly met
richer and more influential people less satisfied with their lives"
(202). Cy lets this pass too, but then she asks, "Why does a gifted
man confine himself to the narrowest possibilities of his talent?"
(202). Even patient Cy has had enough. He turns to Seldon and says,

"You know, Seldon, you're my pal. I've seen you taking lots of punishment for
years. It's pained me. Though I know you require a certain amount of suffer-

ing. But do you need this much? I mean what are you going to get out of this lady. If America were between her legs, Columbus would have turned around." I put my palm over Sylvia's opening mouth. "This is a *mouth*." I took it away as her teeth came down. "It's going to tear you apart, Seldon. It's going to bite, and swallow what it wants and spit the rest of you into the street." (202)

This would seem to be a pretty good speech, one that should have restored Cy's wounded male pride, but his great moment is diminished later when he crawls in bed next to his sleeping girlfriend, Emma, and gives her warm "twin interrogations" the "male salute" (204). After he turns away from her, he discovers "the lieutenant still saluting, though now, in confused loyalty, it was saluting another body, the powerful, Seldon-occupied, Sieglinde Fortress that was Sylvia" (204).

Many of the small triumphs scored by Stern's mostly weak men are at the expense of women, either as objects of sexual conquest or as targets of angry, verbal assault. Do these patterns of male behavior in his fiction make Stern a chauvinist? Or is Stern simply being his realist self, devoted to showing not what ought to be but what is? He seems to be saying that this is how the male animal, especially the injured male animal, behaves when it feels low or is under attack, especially when the attacker is a woman. The misogyny of these characters and their insecurity, their volatility and their lust are all connected, all part of living in a world where infrequent victory is hedged by frequent humiliation.

Another way to answer the charge that Stern is a misogynist is to point out that not all the women in his work are pathetic losers like Miss Wilmott and Miss Swindleman, nymphomaniacs like Patricia Davidov, or viragoes like Sylvia. Though Stern clearly admires the fighting spirit of some of his angry men, there are higher rungs in his fiction's hierarchy, and several of them are occupied by women.

Heroic Resolve

Though almost all characters in Stern's short stories suffer defeat and humiliation, and though several of them enjoy at least moments of triumph and pleasure, the best of them achieve a kind of heroic stature not for their propensity for losing or winning but for their willingness to endure. Some endure cheerfully, with courage and resolve. A precious few even profit from their misfortunes; they learn, grow, forgive, become more compassionate and loving. In a review of *Noble Rot* Tom Rogers writes that Stern "is an astoundingly energetic writer, delivering knockout punches that floor his characters, who usually come battling back from the most devastating humiliations and disasters that Stern can devise for them. And he loves that. Vitality and the power to survive seem to be at the very top of Stern's pyramid of values." Rogers later adds, however, that "the explosiveness of these stories is humane, and the vitality and power to survive that Stern admires is never achieved by indifference to others, or by cutting oneself off" (Rogers).

A good illustration of several of these principles can be found in Holleb, the protagonist of "Ins and Outs," who is mugged one afternoon by a black man pretending to collect money for the Biafra relief fund. Holleb is business manager of the *Hyde Park Herald* and also a minor neighborhood celebrity for the Walter Lippmann–style column he writes for that publication. And he is the father of a teenage son turning hippie and husband to a wife who abandoned him to go to California. As he lies in his hospital bed, he takes stock of his life: "his own tally sheet was nothing to carve on granite: Marriage: over. Son: miserable. Apartment: in bad shape. Work: third rate. Books: unwritten. Victimizer: uncaught" (*NR*, 11). Holleb's heroism consists in part in his ability to face the record squarely without flinching, but he is admirable as well for his desire to understand. He empathizes with the pangs of his son's adolescence, even cleans the boy's cave of a room on a regular basis. He seems to have forgiven his wife for abandoning him. He can even empathize with his attacker. The police sergeant fears that when they catch the assailant, Holleb will fail to see the case through a court trial. Holleb concedes the possibility that understanding will equal forgiveness ("*Tout comprendre, tout pardonner*" [12]), but he also knows "the weakness of this fatigued exoneration . . . the evasiveness of easy pardon" (11-12). If they catch his attacker, Holleb thinks that he will "probably, reluctantly, see the darn case through" (12). He takes his social obligations seriously.

Thirty-seven-year-old Charlotte Trowbridge of "In a Word, Trowbridge" also gets mugged, but her mugging takes place in New York, and in a sense, the mugging is merely the impersonal, physical equivalent of what her parents have done to her all her life. Her father, now dead, was the foremost painter of his generation. His name is New England aristocratic, and it is the only thing she can say at first to the policeman after she is found lying on the pavement. Her mother, still alive and also an artist, has suffered all her life from a starved ego; her talent as a mother is starving her daughter of love and self-confidence:

> At first, it was the standard mother-daughter cut-down. Her few friends suf-
> fered similar cuts and, by adolescence, recognized the sexual rivalry. Here,
> though, there was intellectual rivalry as well. Not since her father had raved
> about a kindergarten drawing, which he'd framed and put into his studio, had
> she known anything but dismissal of any accomplishment, drawn, written,
> played, thought out. At best, there was laughter or patronising dismissal of
> "charm," "amateur ease," "sweet," maybe "moving" or "touching." What
> counted was the annihilation of whatever gift the child of two artists would
> more than possibly show. It was a systematic refrigeration which she felt in
> her whole being. (*Shares*, 199-200)

In some ways, Charlotte recalls earlier lonely spinsters like Miss Wilmott and Miss Swindleman. But Charlotte is not defeated in the ways her precursors are. In fact, the mugging seems to strengthen her. "I'm just the age you were when you married," she reminds her mother, "when you and Daddy began doing the best work of your life" (202). Then she silently reminds herself: "Not that she was set-ting up a rivalry. Success was less important than resolve. Success was transient and problematic, resolve was a way of existing. No point in continuity if it wasn't inspired by that" (200).

In "The Ideal Address" and "Troubles" Stern creates other lik-able, strong, sensitive female characters who try to make the best of bad situations. Real estate agent Winnie of "The Ideal Address" is the center around which several lives revolve. Abandoned by husband, Frederick, four years after she supported him through eight years of dissertation writing, she remains the pillar in the life of son Freddy, a 24-year-old do-nothing who has inherited his father's "blond charm, the gift of living off women, and – might as well face it – a deep tract of sheer dumbness, a power of self-delusion from which contempt or dislike washed easily" (*NR*, 14). As a "real" estate agent, self-decep-tion does not come easily to Winnie. She also nurses her daughter, Nora, through a hysterectomy and is told by her son-in-law that she is "a brick" (18). Most of her attention, however, goes to her boyfriend, Tom; she moves in with him out of pity after he gets dumped by his psychotherapist. Winnie spurns introspection, as do many of Stern's heroes, preferring a life of quiet suffering as she helps others through their ordeals. Hannah, the protagonist of "Troubles," also accepts suffering as inevitable, but she resolves at the end of her story to separate from her self-centered graduate student husband. She has had enough of the "egocentricity of damaged egos" (*NR*, 123).

In "Riordan's Fiftieth" Stern creates one of his bleakest domestic scenes. Chicago bus driver George Riordan returns home on his fiftieth birthday after a hard day's work, home to a loveless marriage and his indifferent, television-watching twin sons. His two older children, a son and a daughter, are now living away from home; the daughter blames him for not being able to pay for her college education. Riordan is not expecting much of a celebration. He "didn't know if his own kids had been told, but knew if he got a greeting out of her, it would leak out of the side of her moon face and make him feel, 'Who're you, Riordan, that anyone in the world should care you've weighted the planet fifty years?'" (*NR*, 316). As it turns out, his wife, Elly, has forgotten. When he tells everyone that it is his birthday, she claims it slipped her mind; she thought it was next week. Then she adds, "And may the next fifty see you try harder" (323). Riordan lets the invitation to another argument pass. Instead he takes the twins out for ice cream. When Riordan gets back, he learns that his son Stan has called to wish him "returns of the day," which pleases him, and that evening he watches the Blackhawks on television. Bobby Hull gets the hat trick (i.e., three goals in one game). Riordan thinks to himself, "The moral was keep looking and waiting and maybe push it a little here or there, there's enough somewhere to celebrate, and maybe she was right, God knows, he could push harder the next fifty" (323).

This ability to make the best of bad situations, to forgive those who have caused injury, and to grow from adversity is also demonstrated by Powdermaker in "Zhoof" and Mottram in "La Pourriture Noble." After his encounter with the anti-Semitic couple on the train, Powdermaker fantasizes his revenge. And, in fact, he exacts that revenge when he stinks up the sleeping car's lavatory right before the anti-Semite uses it. But Powdermaker also learns about himself,

the evasive shallowness of his life, as a result of the unpleasant incident, and by the end of the story he is also able to acknowledge the
flawed humanity of the couple who slighted him. Derek Mottram's
forgiveness of Denis Selinbon comes in a dream at the end of "La
Pourriture Noble." As Mottram stands with his ex-wife outside his
father's church in England, he hears a child's cry: "It was little
Deirdre [his daughter]. Who was also little Denis. He/she ran
outside into his arms, weeping, and he told her/him, 'I'll never leave
you.' In his body, he felt her/his sobbing relief" (*NR*, 358).

That characters like Charlotte Trowbridge, George Riordan,
Arthur Powdermaker, Derek Mottram, and many others in the Stern
galaxy suffer as they do without losing the ability to love – indeed,
some of them learn to love through suffering – this, for Stern, seems
to be the greatest heroism of all.

Chapter Six

Betrayal

. . . the sheer scale of contemporary deception deserves novel consideration.
(The Chaleur Network, 170)

Betrayal is a recurring theme in Richard Stern's novels and stories. It is a subject he explores in great depth, and from a number of perspectives, ranging from that of the victims of betrayal to that of the betrayers themselves. He displays the effects of various kinds of treason, both public and private, and he analyzes the almost endless causes of such actions. The plots of many of his fictions – especially in the early novels *Golk* and *Europe: Or Up and Down with Baggish and Schreiber* – hinge on acts of deception and disloyalty. One of the ironies of the latter novel is that the rising Baggish continually uses Schreiber without the declining Schreiber ever realizing it. Even though Baggish sees Schreiber as "a bridge to the fortress he [Baggish] had to take" (128) and therefore manipulates the older American at will, Baggish pretends that he is innocent in the ways of the world and even asks Schreiber to "give him tips here and there" (124). Schreiber never discovers that Baggish reads a top-secret cable on Schreiber's desk and uses the classified information to get a job as a foreign correspondent for an American newspaper; Schreiber is later investigated for the leak. Baggish is not the only one to betray poor Schreiber. The two European women with whom Schreiber falls in love, Micheline in Versailles and Traudis in Heidelberg, both run off with his former army driver, Tiberius.

Golk's strategy with his show "You're on Camera" is to trick his subjects into revealing their absurdities and vices to millions of television viewers. When the show's popularity increases, Golk uses deception to expose important government and union officials who have betrayed the public's trust. The final twist to the betrayal theme in *Golk*, however, comes when Hendricks and Hondorp agree with virtually no hesitation to replace Golk on "You're on Camera." Hondorp rationalizes his treason by claiming the change will be good for Golk as well as the show. Hendricks, the more honest of the two, recognizes that she seeks a new form of knowledge: "Treason, the betrayal of Golk, was, in the long run, what she was, or so she thought, after. She entered into it not despite, but because of the special pain it caused. Feeling Hondorp's hand in hers, she said, as if prompted from the statue's heroic voice, 'The world was all before her.' The remark sprang from her lifelong devotion to the cult of experience. There was still something new to do and feel" (171-72). One of the experiences Hendricks's treason leads to, of course, is a tongue lashing from Golk:

> "The cesspool cover is off, eh? For weeks, you've been accumulating your stink, and now I see what it looks like. Why didn't I smell it earlier? You've been walking through this office like the plague, and I didn't see it till now. Look at you, the whiteness of the whale. You leper. And here," with a long finger at Hondorp, "here's the licker of your festers, drunk on your pus. You two, Judas and Mrs. Judas. You lousy, four-flushing stinkers. What am I wasting my guts on you for?" (178)

Hendricks, in other words, gets her money's worth for her betrayal; Hondorp gets more than he ever imagined.

In Search of Honor

Stern confronts the issue of betrayal even more directly in his third novel, *In Any Case* (1962; republished as *The Chaleur Network* in 1981). The book was inspired by a factual account of a World War II spy ring, Jean Overton Fuller's *Double Webs* (1958). While writing her book, according to Stern, Fuller "discovered the man who she felt betrayed the group to the Germans. At the end of the book, she looks him up and confronts him with her evidence. He denies it, and that's that" (Raeder, 171). Stern develops a similar plot for *The Chaleur Network*. "What interested me was treason . . . ," Stern has said. "My interest was in the relationship between the traitor and the discoverer, and I worked out an intrigue in which the discoverer finds in himself a treasonous impulse which is related to the official traitor's" (Raeder, 171-72).

When the novel opens in 1948, American businessman Samuel Curry has lived and worked in France for 30 years. He came as an artillery officer at the end of World War I, married a French woman, and went into the steel manufacturing business with his wife's brother. Now 57, Curry lives comfortably alone in Paris. His wife, Hélène, died several years earlier from a wound in her thigh – a wound she inflicted after a public quarrel with Curry. His son, Bobbie, was killed five years earlier at Auschwitz. One day Curry's quiet, self-indulgent existence is shattered when he receives in the mail a book written by a Jesuit priest, Father Trentemille, that accuses Bobbie of betraying to the Germans the Chaleur Network, the resistance group to which Bobbie belonged.

Samuel Curry has been a narcissist and in some respects a coward – certainly not a man of action – all his life. Yet he resolves to investigate the Chaleur Network and exonerate his son. For one thing, Curry is convinced of Bobbie's honor: "While he lived," writes Curry, "he was largely an unknown quantity to me, yet I felt surer than I felt anything about myself that he was incapable of betrayal, that he had bravery built into him, that the virtues I lacked, he had" (*CN*, 12). Curry undertakes the investigation to clear both his conscience and Bobbie's name, for Curry had been a philandering husband and "a terrible father" (1). On the one occasion he considers the possibility that his son was a traitor, Curry blames himself:

> if, say, Bobbie had stumbled into what I knew was an un-Bobbien action, might it not be an action that was older than he himself, one that was mine? Was there not in my life a streak of treason, one which appeared under the private forms of betraying my wife and romping over Bobbie? Official treason, like disease, is but the hot version of the war whose hostilities existed for years without official recognition. . . . Could Bobbie's public "treason," if it turned out that there was actual treason, be the spilling out into his life of the evasions which characterized mine . . . ? (42)

After Curry tracks down various members of the network, he is in fact able to prove his son's innocence. Even after he finds the evidence that will clear Bobbie's name, however, he persists in the investigation. In retrospect he realizes that "it was my own need that did not want the case to end, that my own case had not been settled, my own defecting had not been tried" (90).

As Curry investigates he learns that Bobbie was the victim of mis-
taken identity. The network had been betrayed by a double agent, a
man named Jean-François Arastignac, whose code name was
"Robert." In writing his account of the spy ring, Father Trentemille
apparently confused the code name with Bobbie's Christian name.
Curry is clearly relieved by his discovery: "Bobbie had been possibly
guilty; now someone else was guilty. That finished Trentemille" (77).
The clarity that Curry enjoys, however, is short-lived. Curry learns
that Arastignac's guilt is problematic. After the war the double agent
was declared innocent of treason by a French tribunal. Although he
did betray the Chaleur Network, Arastignac claimed to have done so
on orders from England so that a more important espionage group
could continue to operate.

Another ambiguity – one never explicitly acknowledged by Curry
but suggested more than once to the reader – is the uncanny resemblance between Arastignac and Curry, despite the obvious difference
that one is a man of action, the other a man of thought. When
Arastignac is first described, for example, we learn that "on the surface, he was impressive. Very well-dressed, polite, soft-spoken,
sprightly, obviously intelligent. There was something spirited about
him, *lustig*, not the least ostentatious. He seemed a man used to
being attended to. He was businesslike but unrushed, even courtly.
He made a very agreeable personal impression. But I knew what he
was, a schemer, a traitor, a liar, a rank adventurer. . . . I doubt if he
cared about anything more than saving his skin. . . . [S]omeone
devoid of principle" (76). Parts of this description certainly sound
like the sophisticated, pampered Curry who during the war refused
to let resistance fighters meet at his country house because he feared
for his safety.

A second description of Arastignac also reminds the reader of
Curry's worst qualities: "He was as mean-spirited a man as I've ever
come upon, a man utterly without scruples, offensive in person, corrupt in morals. He would have sold out anyone for a few francs. His
chief characteristic, in my opinion, was a boundless ego which put
itself above cause, country, fellow-man, or God" (81). Though Curry
can hardly be called "mean-spirited," he has all his life put himself
before others. Thus the initially misleading confusion of Bobbie and
"Robert" progresses to the more apt and more disturbing doubling
of Samuel Curry and Arastignac.

Stern has said that his strategy in the novel is to keep reversing the reader's expectations, perhaps in order to approximate the unpredictable, morally opaque world of espionage (Raeder, 172). Just when Curry thinks he has arrived at the truth about the network, for example, he discovers that Arastignac may not have been a traitor after all but a double agent acting in concert with British intelligence. Another unexpected complication occurs when Curry meets and falls in love with Jacqueline Bargouille, who had been both a member of the spy group and Bobbie's lover. Curry in a sense takes his dead son's place in the network and with his son's girlfriend, who moves to Paris and into Curry's apartment. The guilty father must then ask if he has once again betrayed his son. After making love with Jacqueline for the first time, Curry wrestles with his bad conscience, persuading himself that he alone is not to blame, that the act of love is collaborative. Besides, he says to himself, "Who lays down the law? Nature's what happens. I love through and with this son. This son is dead. Burn out a bulb, replace it. I bring love. That's not hate. Love adds, not soils. Who's hurt?" (159).

Jacqueline's conscience, however, is not so easily assuaged. She tells him that she has decided to move out of his apartment: "You're his father, dead or alive. Relationships don't alter with death; only the way you feel about them alters. He was my lover. I can't enjoy with his father what I should be enjoying with him. You took so much of his pleasure in life, and now you want it after he's gone. You've always had it, young, middle-aged, and now. When will you stop just having pleasure?" (166). Curry protests that he loves her, but fearing that her real motive for wishing to leave is their difference in age, he agrees to their separation.

With Jacqueline gone from his apartment, Curry once again picks up his investigation. He discovers that Arastignac is living in Paris and is even listed in the phone book. Curry writes the double agent a note inviting him to explain his actions during the war. When Arastignac arrives at Curry's apartment, the angry father confronts the man who betrayed his son: "You sent men who depended on your faithfulness to their death. You sold out. You were a Judas. Why, I don't know. I'd like to know. You're sitting now in the parlor of a man who will never see his only son because you did what you did" (173). Arastignac tells Curry that he has "missed the heart of the affair" (174) and explains that Bobbie's network was a "smoke screen for regular intelligence. In a showdown, the special operation was to yield to the regular one" (175). Curry seems to accept this explanation; in fact, the two men strike up a friendship, and before long Arastignac asks Curry to work for his air transport business. Curry, who has been in retirement, agrees.

The plot twists again when Curry introduces Arastignac to Jacqueline, and soon the two men find themselves in competition for her love. One afternoon Arastignac takes Curry for a ride in a plane and spins the craft upside down for a loop-de-loop. Curry wonders if his rival is trying to kill him. When they are on the ground Arastignac confesses to sending Curry Father Trentemille's book. Curry can only conclude that Arastignac did so "to inflict pain, to distribute his own pain, to parcel out his personal treason" (203). In a later scene the two men square off about Jacqueline. Arastignac says that she is with Curry as "a souvenir of what meant most to her" but that now "she needs something else, someone else, someone who doesn't have an invisible Siamese twin at his side, who isn't knitted to a corpse" (218). Curry asks what makes Arastignac think "she can live in the same bed with the man who took the real love of her life out of it? And then forced out the nearest thing to love she's had since?" (219). Curry tells the younger man to leave Jacqueline alone. Arastignac responds that "the woman's not a hot water bottle" (220).

The scene ends inconclusively, as does the novel. Curry brings new charges against Arastignac, and once again the double agent is exonerated by the French courts. But at least Curry has managed to get a letter of retraction from Father Trentemille about the charges against Bobbie published in Le Monde. Meanwhile, Curry and Jacqueline have married and moved to the Riviera. She is four months pregnant, but Curry is not sure if the child is his. It could be Arastignac's, or someone else's. One mark of how much Curry has changed is that the uncertainty does not seem to bother him. He seems to have learned to love without egotism.

What, then, has Curry learned about the causes of treason? Some people become traitors out of self-interest, desire for money and advancement. Or they become traitors because they lack a commitment to any principle except self-preservation, getting by from day to day. Or they lack the strength of character to hold fast to what they know they should believe in; they lack tenacity. "Treason," writes

Curry, "I looked it up – from *traditio*, a giving up" (221). Recalling a
time when he betrayed his wife and his best friend by sleeping with
that friend's wife – "a clear case of unrestraint" (131) – Curry
reflects, "Simple double-dealing and treachery don't need malice for
guidance. Stupidity, feebleness, arrogance, maybe even high intelligence can guide people into it. There are just fewer actions in the
world than there are sources of action" (132). Sometimes, to keep
faith with one side of himself, a person must betray another side.
Sometimes the smaller cause (or spy network) must be sacrificed,
betrayed, for the sake of the larger. *The Chaleur Network* explores
the twisted allegiances of a fallen world – a world in which all are
inevitably guilty and honor is rare. In finding selfless love at 60, in
facing up to his earlier sins as a husband and father, and in accepting
the moral complexities of the modern world, Curry comes closer to a
kind of honor than he has ever come before.

Sexual Treasons

In their final confrontation scene Arastignac mentions to Curry a
book about Guatemalan Indians who "worship not only Jesus, but
Judas Iscariot" (217). When Curry says that Arastignac mentions this
practice to excuse himself for his own treasons, the latter responds,
"Is it right for you to speak from the judge's bench? . . . My book says
that the Judas god was invented to take care of sexual guilt. Here's
where all real treason occurs, where the temptations are strong and
the taboos also. The Indian world is harrowed by adultery and all
kinds of license. The Judas god marks the end of passion, and he
expiates their guilt" (218).

Curry understands that these comments are directed at his many
sexual infidelities; he counters that such offenses are nothing compared with "setting your colleagues up in the shooting gallery"
(218). Curry, of course, is right. There is a big difference between
shooting people and committing adultery, a big difference between
treason against a nation and treason with one's neighbor's wife.
Nevertheless, the impulses behind the two kinds of betrayal, if not
the consequences, are related, and Curry is certainly guilty of sexual
betrayal. He has not only committed adultery with Vilette, his best
friend's wife; on the day that his wife, Hélène, is buried, Curry,

standing at the edge of her grave, confesses, "I looked up at Phebe Delattre [one of his mistresses], in black with a half-veil over her perfect face, and indicated that I would see her as soon as the funeral was over" (95).

The list of adulterers in Stern's fiction is many times longer than his list of professional spies. If Curry stands out as a philanderer, it is less for the number of his offenses than for the depth of his long-after-the-fact shame. He gets some help with his self-condemnation when he accuses Phebe of betraying Bobbie to the Germans (she had had an affair with a Nazi officer), and she explodes in angry self-defense: "You're a traitor, a swine. . . . Was I to kill Bobbie? Are you telling me I killed Bobbie? Look at yourself, you, famous all over Paris for your disregard of him. Your women – me, brought and flaunted in front of him. It's you who knocked him down. You couldn't stand anyone in your way. You were made to be alone. Lying with me, moaning over me, you were always by yourself, loving nothing but Sam. The American, Uncle Sam, free and alone" (145). Phebe's puzzling suggestion of political allegory in Curry's name aside, the speech hits Curry hard, though not as hard as he hits himself elsewhere in the novel.

Some of Stern's sexual transgressors go about their task with joyful abandon. If the illicit nature of their actions is a factor at all, it is as an enhancer of pleasure. The fear of getting caught, the thrill of violation, the taste for forbidden fruit often seem to propel Stern's wrongdoers into action. When Edward Gunther sleeps with Nina for the first time in *Stitch*, he feels a few qualms because she is drunk and does not know what she is doing, and because he knows the last thing Nina consciously wants is sexual passion. He justifies his act by telling himself, "How would she know anything if she didn't know she was capable of this? He'd been of use to her. She'd see it" (*Stitch*, 75). But Edward does not have a guilty thought to spare for his wife, Cressida, who waits for him at home in their apartment with the children. Nina, when she sobers up, shows more of a bad conscience: "To have had her own quick way, knocking over whoever stood there. Cressida, whose hurt she'd seen, in whose home she'd had happy hours" (80).

Later, in Rome, Edward picks up a young American woman, Sibyl, and exults in his good fortune: "This girl was made to be his. Open, educable, unrancorous, a beauty. A little too young but what did that count? That was abstraction. He loved this city, this girl, Italy, his own puzzlement, his own useless, granular life. Precious life, that so muddled a portion of it could contain such thoughts, such pleasures. Oh, you groaning commentators, loud-mouthed worriers, relax, rest, be pure, let time take you where it will" (148). The passage continues with Edward promising himself "no more hiding, disguising. Make the grain of things your own. Honesty is therapy" (148). Yet Edward is never so honest as to confess to Cressida the details of his Roman holiday.

Composer Jeffrey Wendt also prefers basking in the pleasures of a lascivious, adulterous bed to wallowing in the guilt his wife prepares for him. He describes himself as "holding off from that puritan, judaic, masochistic analysis which will show me as tyrant, betrayer and brute, and will see Velia as Ariel calibanized by me" (*Shares*, 86). Another free spirit of this kind is Mervyn Kiest, the unemployed graduate student in "Lesson for the Day." Though Kiest never abandons his lust for Angela Deschay, he does experience a moment of panic when Angela's husband, Jimmy, begins his sermon with Matthew 26:23: "'And he answered and said, He that dippeth his hand with me in the dish, the same shall betray me'" (*NR*, 236). "'Mother Mary,' thinks Kiest. 'Does the bastard know?'" (*NR*, 237). Fortunately for Kiest, Jimmy remains oblivious to the dipping hands around him.

Not every Stern adulterer is joyful, of course. In addition to the retroactively guilty Samuel Curry, there is Robert Merriwether, the protagonist of *Other Men's Daughters*, who suffers the transformation from "low-keyed, middle-aged prof softened by American life and Harvard cream" to "Burgher Outlaw gripped by passion for a girl a year older than his son" (41). Merriwether at least has his reasons for looking elsewhere; his marriage to Sarah had dried up years before he meets the young woman who stirs him. Justified or not, Merriwether feels miserable about the dishonesty and betrayal he perpetrates. Less justified, and perhaps for that reason far more remorseful, are Susannah Wursup and Will Eddy, the ex-wife and best friend of protagonist Fred Wursup in *Natural Shocks*. For two years they carried on an affair behind Wursup's back (he never does find out). The affair, we learn, was "savaged . . . by shame and farce" (122). Will learns to cope with his guilt through psychoanalysis. He is also "a serious Catholic convert, a needling conservative, a man who relished the notion of sin and his own capacity for it" (120). Susannah does not have the benefit of therapist or religion to ease her bad faith: "She got away with it; so she paid through the nose and kept paying" (206).

So much for the betrayers. Stern is just as interested in the betrayed. "The fear of, the agony of betrayal of those close to one," Stern has said. "That's a powerful feeling" (Appendix). Some Stern characters are both betrayers and betrayed. Samuel Curry, at least, suffers jealousy at the thought of Jacqueline and Arastignac being together; he even suffers the paranoid, but possibly accurate, fear that Arastignac tries to kill him when he turns his small plane upside down. Curry must endure the kind of pain he once inflicted on others; he is made to pay in his own coin. By the end of the novel he seems to have learned how to cope with uncertainty. "Much of what happiness I have," he says, "is connected with marriage to Jacqueline, but I have resolved to let her do what she wants. What else is there to do? Shoot her?" (*CN*, 241).

Few of Stern's characters handle the fear, much less the fact, of betrayal so well. In *Europe* Schreiber weeps in the back of a taxi (and is consoled by the driver) after he learns that Micheline has run off with Tiberius. The reaction to betrayal is more aggressive in *Golk*. When he learns that Hendricks and Hondorp have agreed to replace him, Golk vomits on network executive Lurcher's expensive carpet. Then Golk plots his revenge. The treason against Golk, of course, is not sexual, though the two traitors become lovers – a fact that suggests a relationship between treason and erotic arousal. After each of the two adulterous meetings between Gunther and Nina in *Stitch*, Stern presents Cressida's point of view. On the first occasion Cressida does not yet know of the affair. Nevertheless, we learn of other ways in which she feels let down by her husband. When she first knew him, he seemed "really something . . . smiled all the time, darted around like a big bird, full of light remarks and answers for things" (78). Her first indication that Edward was not all that he seemed came two weeks before their wedding when she learned of Adrienne, his first wife: "She should have thought then about whatever defect had let him conceal such a thing from a fiancée. What was too hard he ran from" (78).

After Cressida sees Nina and Edward racing through the streets of Venice, the lid flies off the cauldron of the neglected wife's rage:

"Out. Out. G-e-t o-u-t. You know. You know what you've been doing. You and that smelly poet. I'm so fed up I can't. Get out!" (120). She throws a shoe and hits him in the ear; he retaliates by throwing a book at her stomach: "She grunted, terribly, and then, more terribly, laughed" (121). Stern follows a similar strategy of presenting the injured wife's point of view in *Other Men's Daughters*. Sarah Merriwether's anger is not just at her husband's adultery but also at the way that she has for years sacrificed her needs to his. She had felt attracted to other men, but had never once been unfaithful. And for her fidelity, her husband humiliates her with an affair that winds up getting publicized in *Newsweek*. No longer would she tolerate being treated like "an interior broom," "a human vacuum cleaner" (138, 139).

In "Double Charley" Stern plays out the theme of sexual treason and the betrayal of friendship in a comic key. The collaborative songwriting team of Charley Schmitter and Charley Rangel had a few hits but nothing for seven years because Schmitter, who lives in New York, has stopped writing lyrics. Rangel, who lives in Chicago, cannot compose without his partner. His only consolation is his on-again, off-again relationship with Maggie and her daughter Chippie. After living with him for five years she leaves him one day to go to New York: "That had been dark-night-of-the-soul time for him" (*NR*, 307). But within a year she and her daughter were back in Chicago, back in Rangel's apartment. But still no lyrics from Schmitter. Maggie keeps telling Rangel that Schmitter will revive himself to write again, and, although Rangel knows the collaboration is over, he continues to hope "until the last day" (312), the day Schmitter dies. Riding from the funeral with his partner's widow, Rangel learns the ugly truth that when Maggie went to New York, she went to Schmitter. Rangel's grief turns to anger and cynicism; he feels his "head cracking" at "the stinking small grain of this world" (314). Schmitter has left Rangel no lyrics: "Here in New York, Double Charley's last song began, the mean act of betrayal that was Charley Rangel's to set, to live with. 'I'da punched his goddamn nose for him,' he said. 'I'd've bloodied the big bastard's nose'" (314).

Assimilation and Its Discontents

There is no question, then, that betrayal is an important theme in Stern's work. Accounting for that importance, however, is altogether another matter. One kind of explanation might look to Stern's experiences as a betrayer. Perhaps he suffers from a guilty conscience. For someone of Stern's moral sensitivity, someone who, like Fred Wursup in *Natural Shocks*, aspires to be a "decent person" (53), every act of treason against another person is simultaneously a self-betrayal. Or perhaps Stern has been hurt by loved ones and friends, and this pain has caused his fascination with the human capacity for deception, which is related to the limited human capacity to know what goes on inside another person's heart or mind. In a universe of partial knowledge, of ourselves as well as others, we must trust. And where there is trust there is always the possibility of bad faith, broken promises, and disillusionment. There are no doubt Freudian explanations as well – Oedipal traumas and sibling rivalries, ways his parents disappointed him or he them. There are hints of strained feelings of this kind in some of Stern's autobiographical fictions about his parents, especially in stories like "Dr. Cahn's Visit" and "Packages."

An equally plausible explanation for Stern's concern with betrayal might be found in his complex attitude toward being a Jew. As an outsider, Stern inherited from his parents and grandparents the intense desire to assimilate. It is this need to belong that caused Stern to claim, when he was at Chapel Hill, that he was half-gentile, and perhaps too it partially explains his love of Europe, his yearning to be a citizen of the world. A citizen of the world belongs to no country, has no racial or ethnic or religious boundaries. Concomitant with this intense desire to assimilate, however, is intense anger at, and fear of, exclusion. And then there is the temptation to self-loathing, either as Jewish anti-Semitism or as self-contempt for denying his Jewishness.

In his life as in his fiction Stern has frequently demonstrated a tendency, perhaps even a need, to get close to the betrayer – often with the desire to confront him in outrage but also with the desire to understand and, if possible, forgive. Stern lived and worked in Germany less than five years after the end of World War II. It is difficult to imagine that there were many Jews, even in the U.S. Army, who were thus situated. In more than one work of fiction characters try to sort out how they feel about what took place there. Henry (formerly "Heinz") Pfeiffer, the Jewish protagonist of "The Good European," immigrated to America to escape the Nazis. When he gets the chance to return to Germany after the war he is understandably ambivalent about what he sees: "He was not unpleased by the destruction. On the other hand, he was not displeased by the construction projects going on over most of the city. 'They can begin again too,' was his notion" (*NR*, 85).

In *Europe* Schreiber listens attentively as Traudis recalls how, as a girl, she loved Hitler; for her there were times when the war seemed "wonderful." She asks Schreiber if he can understand that, and he responds, thinking of his own pleasant war experiences in Versailles, "I think I can, Traudis. . . . I can understand it" (173). Samuel Curry of *The Chaleur Network* says that his credo is "that old line 'understanding all is forgiving all'" (65). When he visits August Mettenleiter, who had served the Nazis as an interpreter during the war, Curry first asks, "as an indispensable preface to vital communication, the question everyone must want to ask the Germans, Why? Was it fear? Lethargy? Ignorance? Belief in a genuine humanitarian version of the program, a purified Europe revitalising heroic legacies?" (72). Later in the book, of course, Curry confronts Arastignac, the man whose lies sent his son to Auschwitz: "Why did you do it, Robert [with Arastignac's permission, Curry calls the former spy by his code name, "Robert"]? What cruelty. You're a good man. You're a kind, a considerate fellow. . . . I know you're good. You have my boy's smile. You're good, as he was. Fifty times better than I" (208). Arastignac can only answer, "I didn't have to do it. . . . I did it. I lived from one minute to the next. That's it. I wasn't afraid. I wasn't cold or hungry. I don't explain it. That'll have to be there between us" (209).

The pattern of confronting the traitor can also be observed in Stern's life in his relationship with Ezra Pound in Venice in the early 1960s. Stern's admiration for Pound's poetry is perhaps the only reason that he sought the old man's acquaintance. But Pound was also a convicted traitor, guilty of broadcasting anti-Semitic tirades. In "A Memory or Two of Pound" Stern writes,

We never talked directly about Jews. His anti-Semitism had been – I think – a wicked rhetorical habit, part populist, part the casual snobbery of upper-middle-class Europe and America. During his worst days, it was reinforced by the slime fury dredged up by the Nazis. It was attached to his historically flawed notions of usury and, now and then, to that nineteenth-century ortho-doxy which had a Hebraic cast. Miss Rudge spoke deliberately of his Jewish friends, and I noted the dedication of *Guide to Kulchur* (to Bunting and Zukofsky). I doubt that he had ever prejudged a human being or a work on racial grounds.

But who knows? (*IR*, 7)

When Pound rudely exploded at Stern during an afternoon tea at Pound's house, it probably crossed Stern's mind that the attack was prompted by anti-Semitism. At least this is one of the things Gunther thinks – but then rejects – after a similar attack from the Pound-like sculptor Stitch: "Is this madness," thinks Gunther. "Anti-semitism? Fascism? . . . Chicago Semite *Venitien*? Not that. That was too easy" (*Stitch*, 61). Proof of Stern's reluctance to accept that Pound was motivated by religious bigotry is that, years later, Stern was deeply surprised and distressed to read about the extent of Pound's anti-Semitism in a book by Robert Casillo.[1]

Many of these issues of anti-Semitism and betrayal are contained in Stern's powerful short story "Zhoof." Though there are many dif-ferences between Stern and his protagonist, Arthur Powdermaker, the experience with an anti-Semitic couple on a train in Europe hap-pened to Stern (Appendix). Like his author, Powdermaker is the "son and grandson of assimilated German-Jewish burghers, his slogans were theirs: let sleeping dogs lie; don't cry over spilt milk" (*NR*, 302). Like Stern, Powdermaker was not bar mitzvahed because his father thought it a waste of money. And like Stern, Powdermaker is an ambitious traveler, a self-styled citizen of the world. When he hears the word "zhoof" something horrible detonates within him:

Zhoof. "Am I so clearly that? The eyes? The big nose? My walk? My open mouth – the Whiner's deferential mouth, the Ingratiator's smile? All the helpfulness with the train; damn eagerness to belong? Jewiness. *Zhoofheit*. Whatever the bastard saw, felt. And couldn't bear. Some yidstuff leaking out of me. The only thing that counted for him. Not tourist, not American, not fellow traveler. Certainly not fellow-man. *Zhoof*. *Disjectamembra*. Garbage." (*NR*, 303)

In being confronted with the anti-Semite, Powdermaker is forced to confront his own self-loathing. The painful experience brings him to a much deeper understanding and acceptance of himself: "Powdermaker had spent his life posing, and would leave behind nothing but a few images that persuaded people to decorate the surface of their lives. Now, thanks to a twisted fellow, he'd been forced into the part of himself that he'd covered over, one it was necessary to recognize, if not defend" (304-5). When he gets off the train at the Gare du Nord in Brussels, Powdermaker exchanges glances with the anti-Semite's wife: "He gave her a small nod, a sympathetic, a human nod. She understood" (305).

For Stern, beyond the rage at betrayal lies the challenge to understand it, to learn from it, and, when possible, to forgive it.

Chapter Seven

Autobiographical Fictions of Love

> . . . why do some of these writers have to draw on their own intimate lives, on the people they know best, those whom they love? Why do they write about their own love affairs, children, divorces, the lives and deaths of their closest friends? ("Inside Narcissus," *IR*, 187)

One of the ironies of Richard Stern's being known as an autobiographical writer is that in the early part of his career he took pride in not writing about himself or those closest to him. "In the first ten or fifteen years of my writing life," Stern said in a 1980 interview, "I was almost always gripped by stories which were 'out there.' I could see them more or less complete even though I might not know the end of the one I began" (Anderson, 99). Reviewers noticed. Peter Buitenhuis praised Stern for not writing about himself, even though he felt *In Any Case* suffers from Stern's "attempt to project himself into a viewpoint character [Samuel Curry] whose experience seems to be larger than, and alien to, his own."[1] Most American novelists, Buitenhuis stated, "rely on autobiography and, as a result, either repeat themselves or dry up." Another critic who noticed a distance between Stern and many of his protagonists in works before 1965 is Frederick Crews. In a review of *Teeth, Dying and Other Matters* Crews stated that "Teeth," "Wanderers," and "Dying" "would be the envy of any contemporary writer"; nevertheless, he added that "the memorable stories are invariably those dealing with insignificant little people from whom Stern is intellectually detached." By "holding his material at arm's length," Crews charged, "Stern risks triviality."[2]

Most of the characters in the novels *Golk*, *Europe*, and *In Any Case*, as well as in most of the stories in *Teeth, Dying and Other Matters*, bear little resemblance to their creator, but these works contain a few brief instances of self-portraiture, mostly satirical. For example, Stern admits to a comic self-portrait in *Europe* in the figure of Frank Horstmann, an American Lektor in Heidelberg who gives a party attended by Schreiber, Baggish, Traudis, and others. When Schreiber arrives early at Horstmann's apartment his host, "a big young man with huge features stuck on a narrow head," is about to sit for supper and asks Schreiber to join him, though he warns his guest that his wife is "not very good with food" (130-31). After Horstmann noisily wolfs down his bratwurst, he begins to talk:

> He addressed Schreiber as if he were speaking to a class of four hundred college sophomores; the room bowed with his eloquence. The topics ranged from the products associated with the names of Chateaubriand and Chesterfield to Professor Oken's theory of cranial structure. Horstmann was a polymath. Schreiber could barely keep afloat . . . . Suddenly, happily, Horstmann, in the midst of an anatomical comparison of the cranium and pelvis, was interrupted by a knock at the door. (132)

Horstmann shares with later self-representations a usually silent, long-suffering wife (whose cooking the husband ridicules), a love of arcane knowledge, and an enthusiasm about sharing that knowledge with others, usually in the form of lectures.

Autobiographical Fiction

Stern had theorized about writers writing fiction about their lives long before he began to write about his. In his essay "Proust and Joyce Underway: The Tradition of Autobiography," first published in *Kenyon Review* in the summer of 1956, Stern identifies autobiographical fiction as a distinctly twentieth-century genre, related to changing conceptions of character:

> The notion of the unknowability of character helped to do away with that standard eighteenth- and nineteenth-century novel which depended on the clash of more or less fixed characters around central figures, who become at the end of the novel more or less like one of the fixed figures. When the new conception undermined this form of the novel, many serious writers turned to "autobiographical fiction." Not that writers could know themselves better than they could know others, but at least they knew what they felt, remembered, and believed. This was material for a novel whose chief technical problem would be the position of the narrator-protagonist. (*FH*, 231).

At the end of the essay Stern speaks of the autobiographical novel as an exhausted form – one depleted by the genius of Proust and Joyce. For these two twentieth-century giants the "exhibition of the writer criticizing his work as he forms it provides a logical conclusion to the tradition of 'autobiography'" (234).

The question of when Richard Stern first made a conscious decision to use his own life as the basis of his fiction is difficult to answer precisely, as are the corresponding questions about why he first did so. Though some of Stern's comments would place his shift from material "out there" to autobiographical material a few years later than 1965, it seems clear that Edward Gunther, the protagonist of *Stitch* (1965), marks a turning point in Stern's practice as a writer.[3] Not only does Gunther's bad experience with Stitch parallel Stern's with Pound, but Gunther's Europhilia and troubles of the marriage bed also seem close to Stern's. At least the harsh, bitter tones of spousal rancor are rendered with inspired authenticity of dialogue and detail. To see Gunther as a turning point, of course, is not to see him as identical with his creator. Edward has a different profession (as do all of Stern's later autobiographical protagonists) – actually he has no profession for most of the novel – and he is made worse than his maker in many ways. His faults, especially his aimlessness and gluttony, are exaggerated beyond recognition of anything in Stern. Still, he is closer to Stern than the protagonists of the author's earlier novels. One thing that perhaps disguises this fact is that Gunther is not the most important character in *Stitch*; though he is a center of consciousness through which most of the novel is filtered, the real magnet of interest is the genius figure, Thaddeus Stitch.

Why did Stern turn to a protagonist like himself in *Stitch*? The change may have been a response to critics like Frederick Crews and Granville Hicks. In a review of *Teeth, Dying and Other Matters* Hicks had written that Stern was a writer of "obvious talent" but worried that Stern "seems to lack a center" and was "either unwilling or unable to show us where he really lives."[4] Stern, however, denies that he was reacting to critics; it was simply a case, he claims, of not being able to write about anything else (Appendix). In a 1980 interview in the *Chicago Review* Stern explained the shift as having to do "with the desire not to restrict [himself], restrict [his] intellect or . . . emotional capacities" (Anderson, 99). Stern's essay "Inside Narcissus" elaborates on this point: "The fiction writer who wants his work to be a source of truth as well as diversion, beauty, merriment, whatever, may be unable to cut himself off from those situations which have affected him most deeply, and those situations may be impossible to detach from those who figured in them" (*IR*, 187-88). The encounter with Pound obviously affected Stern deeply. The "emotional aftermath," he has stated, led him to write *Stitch* (*FH* 292). Stern seems also to have been affected deeply by problems in his marriage, and these too found an outlet in his art.

Though works like *Stitch, Veni, Vidi . . . Wendt, Other Men's Daughters, Natural Shocks,* and *A Father's Words* originate in Stern's life experiences, the goal is never merely to report or record those experiences. Instead, his experiences are the materials he transmutes into art. If anything, Stern goes out of his way to dislocate himself from the autobiographical origins of his plots. He changes the number, ages, and sexes of the children – and the hair color of the wife – in each work. Most important of all, Stern changes the profession of the protagonist – a practice often providing a rich technical vocabulary that "will suggest certain habits of mind," image patterns, and settings that he works into the narrative (*IR*, 189). Thus Gunther is an ex–advertising copywriter. Jeffrey Wendt of *Veni, Vidi . . . Wendt* is a composer. Robert Merriwether of *Other Men's Daughters* is a professor of physiology and a physician; Frederick Wursup of *Natural Shocks* is a journalist. Cyrus Riemer of *A Father's Words* edits a science newsletter. The autobiographical stories offer a similar range of professions for the protagonists: for example, Marcus Firetuck, the cartographer and amateur poet in "Mail"; Arthur Powdermaker, the photographer's model in "Zhoof"; and Walters, the assistant secretary for economic affairs in the State Department in "In Return."

Stern has at times seemed impatient with readers who search for one-to-one correspondences between a writer's life and art, as if the process of transforming life into art were as simple as photocopying a legal document. In the essay "Events, Happenings, Credibility, Fictions," for example, he writes dismissively of "biographies which draw parallels between the artist's life and his fictional version of it" (*FH*, 100). Because the fiction writer changes "the components of the work of art" to suit "the pattern of his felt insight," he is protected from lawsuits. "A work of imaginative art," Stern continues, "really represents only those moments of an artist's life which were expressible in that period of isolation from the world in which he worked out what counts for him; in the process of working it out, he alters it under pressure of his insight and his form. Places, times, and details which originally stimulated his imagination come to belong more and more to each other, less and less to the world from which they came" (100-101).

A similar impatience with naive interpreters can be found in Stern's fiction. Stitch complains bitterly about the tendency of some critics to see all art, even his island of sculptures, as confession: "Kiss and tell, suffer and yell. One of them tried to make Sant Ilario a diary. A giant Stitch from the gonads up. As if they'd never heard of Greece, Egypt. Know thyself. How that perverted them" (*Stitch*, 85). Wendt opens his narrative, supposedly a diary account of the composition of his opera, with a similar disclaimer: "Any thoughtful man who types the solitary 'I' on the page as much as I have these past weeks must consider its perils. This is a great time for 'I.' Half the works billed as fiction are just sprayed (or styrofoamed) memoirs. . . . I'm not writing autobiography. Nietzsche asks, 'Aren't books written precisely to hide what is in us?' Granting the exceptional concealments of his time, isn't this still the case?" (*Shares*, 45).

Stern would likely say that correspondences between life and art, however fascinating as gossip, are irrelevant to the appreciation of the work of art. And the work of art, he would add, is all that should matter. Then why raise the issue of autobiographical fiction at all? Most twentieth-century writers draw on their own lives to some degree. One reason to raise the issue is that Stern himself has raised it – and raised it brilliantly – on several occasions, in essays and interviews. Besides, Stern is not above searching for autobiographical clues in the works of other artists – his portraits of writers like Robert Lowell and Samuel Beckett, for example, reveal a keen eye for spotting such connections (and discrepancies) between life and art. Despite his own warnings about the dangers of literary gossip, Stern can be as guilty on this count as any of his interpreters.

The Marital Waste Land

Though Stern has not necessarily become more autobiographical with each novel after *Stitch*, there is almost certainly less disguise, less dislocation, in Jeffrey Wendt of *Veni, Vidi . . . Wendt* than in Edward Gunther. With Gunther, Stern transfigured himself from a Fulbright fellow in Italy into an irresponsible American who has quit his job in Chicago and sold his house so that he and his family could live in Europe. With Wendt, Stern transformed himself from an English professor teaching summer school at the University of California at Santa Barbara into composer/music professor Jeffrey Wendt who takes a summer's visiting appointment in music at the same university. If Gunther captures something of Stern's speculative, intellectual side, Wendt captures Stern the artist. And, like his maker, Wendt is also an intellectual, a university (University of Chicago!) composer. His art is as heavily allusive as is Stern's fiction; his work-in-progress, in fact, is an opera based on the life of Horace Walpole. Even Wendt's frustration with his lack of fame resembles that of his author. Wendt describes himself as having "a very small public name" (44) and as having been in a 16-month creative drought (51).

The relationship between husband and wife, and later ex-wife, is a main thread that runs through all the autobiographical fictions. Edward Gunther and Jeffrey Wendt are both unhappily married, and both carry on affairs. Edward actually feels something like love for Nina Callahan, but the feeling, or at least the desire to get involved, is not shared by Nina. Wendt's affair with Patricia Davidov is purely, hilariously sexual, though hatred of Patricia's husband also fuels his passion. In *Stitch* Cressida discovers the affair between Edward and Nina, and the discovery leads to separation and presumably divorce. In *Veni, Vidi . . . Wendt* Velia never discovers her cheating husband, but her complaints about him (and Wendt's unhappiness with her) sound a lot like the unhappy couple in *Stitch*. Part of the problem is that husband and wife in each marriage come from such different, incongruous, incompatible backgrounds. Gunther and Wendt are Jews; Cressida and Velia are not. Gunther abhors Cressida's "culinary viciousness" (*Stitch*, 165); she regards him as "a rolling sack of self-content" (76). There is no longer real intimacy or love between them. At one point Cressida wonders why: "What had happened? Natural attrition? Age? Constricting life? Two lines which had never been parallel diverging more and more? Or maybe it was the institution itself, good for a decade, the rest sufferance?" (79). After she discovers the affair with Nina, even sufferance is out of the question.

Things have not deteriorated to quite the same extent in the
Wendt marriage, largely because Jeffrey Wendt does not get caught
cheating, but this is no ideal pairing either. As with the Gunthers,
religious – or, rather, ethnic – differences are a factor. When
Jeffrey's Aunt Jo, her sisters, and his father visit in Chicago, Velia
provides the food:

> their old hearts are sunk at the thin New England provision, the cellophaned
> corned beef, the thin, pre-sliced rye bread staled in the Protestant markets
> which magnetize Velia, and, for sweets, dry wafers in lieu of the thick snail
> curls of raisins, nuts, and caramelized dough, or the scarlet tarts, the berries
> swillingly augmented by terrific syrups. No, nothing is right, but then how
> should a thin-nosed aristocrat know what keeps old Jews alive? (*Shares*, 50)

Jeffrey, Sr., finds Velia's notebooks scattered about their sublet
house in Santa Barbara; they contain an "epic catalog of [his] smells,
warts, and deformities (hairy toes, unbalanced ass, flabby chest,
hawkish nose – black hair rampant on snotty verdure)" (84). He is
hardly enamored of her looks anymore, either, although when he
sees her in a new dress he thinks the Finnish print "almost restores
her looks. (She had them, her legs are very fine, her body thin, but
neat; but that's over)" (71). When she runs the vacuum outside the
room where he composes, he sneaks up behind her and stamps the
circuit-breaker – an action that sends her weeping into her pillow.
Still, they hold on, stay married, return as a family to Chicago.

Many of the male protagonists in *1968* (1970), the volume in
which *Veni, Vidi . . . Wendt* first appeared, seem, like Wendt, to be
suffering through the banalities and frustrations of mid-life crises.
Those who are married are unhappily married. Others are divorced,
widowed, or abandoned. Almost all of them are lonely, unfulfilled,
and, for the married – if the opportunity arises, unfaithful. Along
with Wendt, perhaps the character closest to Stern is the unnamed
narrator of the piece called "Storymaking," which contains a
description of meeting his friend Al in New York. Al is a thinly veiled
portrait of Philip Roth just after Roth's first wife is killed in an accident in Central Park and months before Roth would publish *Portnoy's Complaint*. As the narrator returns to Chicago, he seems to
reject the solipsistic ways of his soon-to-be-famous friend: "The
minor, low-living burgher, with difficulty still married to the same
wife, deprived of fifty-dollar-an-hour self-revelations, never penis-

threatened with a knife, never easing the needy wand in the family steak, fantasist but not solipsist, story-searcher but, usually, small-time inventor, flies back with his daughter to Chicago" (*1968*, 205).

The low-living burgher would not stay married much longer. Indeed, before *1968* was published in 1970, irreversible changes had already occurred. *Other Men's Daughters* emerged from Stern's affair with Alane Rollings, which began in 1969, and his eventual divorce from Gay Clark Stern in 1972. It is Stern's best-known, most widely translated, and most highly praised novel. In the minds of some readers, especially those who know Gay and Richard Stern, it is also his most controversial novel. Bad enough, the argument goes, to have an affair with a student and turn himself and his family into campus stereotypes, objects of gossip, pity, and ridicule (or perhaps in Stern's case, of envy), but to write a book about the affair is to compound the original offense. Why do it? Did he hope to transform the chaos of painful emotions into something positive, a work of truth and beauty? Was it a way of working through difficult psycho-logical problems? Did he wish to make a public confession of his sins? Or, rather, did he hope to tell his side of the story and thus justify what he had done?

At first glance *Other Men's Daughters* does seem to be organized to get across Stern-the-wrongful-husband's version of events. But this is a very dangerous conclusion, since Stern differs from his pro-tagonist in many important respects. Unlike Stern, or for that matter Edward Gunther and Jeffrey Wendt, all of them assimilated Jews, pro-tagonist Robert Merriwether is a New England blue blood, a Cam-bridge WASP. Like Stern and Wendt, he is a university professor, but unlike those two he is a scientist, a physiologist who has written a "semi-popular book" on thirst. Merriwether is also a physician who moonlights a few hours a week at Harvard's Holyoke Center. The professions of doctor and creative writer, however, are not as far apart as some might imagine. Long ago Merriwether had "sensed an important relationship between the practice of medicine and that of the poets and sages. . . . Many poets had been physicians or the chil-dren of physicians. Dr. Merriwether supposed the connection had to do with the importance of human crisis in both occupations. Doctors and poets had to do with essentials; they knew the confusion and mystery of suffering, the disproportion between the human being as complex chemistry and the human being unmade by death" (15).

Despite this link between doctors and poets, it would be difficult
to argue that Merriwether is more like Stern than is Jeffrey Wendt. If
there is a progression in Stern's autobiographical fictions from one
work to the next, it is not so much one of increasing resemblance to
the author as it is one of Stern's increasing acceptance of and
respect for his protagonists. Certainly, Robert Merriwether's fall into
adultery is presented in the most sympathetic way imaginable. The
40-year-old Harvard professor is alone for the summer in Cambridge
while his wife and four children vacation on Duck Island, Maine. His
marriage to Sarah has been disintegrating for years; for years they
have lived without intimacy, without sex, sharing only their house (a
Merriwether family legacy) and a love for their children. When they
were first married, Sarah had shown a great interest in his work, but
this had proved a pretense: "How long was it before they both realized she not only didn't follow but was bored stiff pretending? Dr.
Merriwether retreated. Then, five or six years ago, Sarah stopped
pretending. She opened a door inside her to a very tough little lady.
The lady said, 'This is it. I am no doormat. You are no Einstein'" (8).
Then, too, Merriwether has begun to have intimations of mortality.
Every morning he reads the *Times* obituary pages, containing "news
of deaths which gripped his heart" (12). He hears Time's chariot
hurrying near.

One day while Merriwether is working at the Holyoke Center a
beautiful young summer school student, Cynthia Ryder, appears in
his office. She wants to renew her prescription for birth control pills.
While Merriwether has his back turned, without his asking, she
removes her dress. Startled by this display, Merriwether tells her he
will not trouble her with an examination. She puts her dress back on,
thanks him, and that appears to end their acquaintance. But he runs
into her on the street twice after their meeting before he realizes he
sees her because "she wanted him to see her" (19). Still, the good
doctor resists. And she persists. She walks him home, even kisses him
on the mouth in public, on the street where he lives. Then, two days
later, she enters his house. Still he resists. At her request he lies
down with her on his daughter's bed, but when she falls asleep, he
gets up and goes into his own bed. But in the morning he finds her
there beside him, naked, pulling down the pants to his pajamas:
"And they became, biologically and legally, lovers" (36).

The affair rejuvenates Merriwether more than even he at first is willing to accept. When the summer session ends he is almost relieved that the ordeal of subterfuge is over. But then, unexpectedly, he receives a postcard from Cynthia, and his passion for her returns with even greater intensity. His friend (and also Sarah's cousin) Timmy Hellman says, "You were thirsty, and you went to the well" (70). Merriwether, the specialist on thirst, responds, "I was thirsty and someone delivered a case of champagne to the door. I hardly knew I was thirsty till it came" (70). Later, Merriwether puts things even more simply to Cynthia's father: "Life surprised me" (119).

If *Other Men's Daughters* celebrates Merriwether's regeneration, it never does so by becoming a facile exercise in male fantasy, or male apologetics. For one thing, after the initial seduction Stern shows Merriwether choosing his fate rather than being merely the object of a young woman's aggressive pursuit. And the choice is not easy. It is accompanied by suffering, guilt, fear, and pity. With one part of himself he struggles against his desire; with another part he yields to it, sees it as a "way out of the prison of . . . feelings" (41). If he feels "poeticized" by Cynthia's love, he also feels "transfigured, en route to restatements of statements he'd lived by, a grotesque, a dirty old man, a standard character for story" (41). One ingredient of the novel's complexity is that we are shown that Merriwether is largely responsible for the lack of intimacy in his marriage, and we are shown this mostly by entering into Sarah's point of view. "You're a terrible person," she tells him after she learns of the affair. "You're a terrible, miserable man" (142). She had given up her intellectual work for him years ago (she had written a master's thesis on courtly love); he had tried to transform her into a cleaning woman. Merriwether concedes as much to a friend: "She feels like the caretaker of a museum nobody visits. And she doesn't like the chief exhibit" (70). Later in the novel, when they get divorced, he writes to a favorite aunt, "I, surely, am most to blame. In her view, I have dominated her and left her no room to be a person" (197).

The novel's romanticism is also tempered by ironies about the relationship between Merriwether and Cynthia – ironies of which Merriwether is fully cognizant. As he gets to know Cynthia better, he realizes the profound depths of her insecurities, her need for male approval. And being the village pariah, the home wrecker on permanent tap for Merriwether, does not help her equilibrium. At times she falls into severe depressions, "screams . . . shrinks into a fetal ball" (153). Against his own nature and inclinations, he learns how to bring her back by kissing her, saying he loves her, even when that is not what he feels. Merriwether tells her father when the two men meet in France that he fears she would harm herself if the relationship were to end. On the other hand, Merriwether fears losing her, worries about the 21-year gap between them. Such fears are not eased when Timmy Hellman warns Merriwether about this new breed of intelligent young woman: "They want, they want, and it's we not-quite-greybeards who give them the most the quickest. We teach them, we spend on them, we show them off, we tell them what everything means. We're their Graduate School. Which means they're closer to graduation through us. And that means there can be lots of tears when Graduation Day rolls around" (71). Perhaps with this warning in mind, Merriwether finds Cynthia an apartment in Cambridge in a building "for old ladies run by old ladies," which leads Cynthia to ask, "Why didn't you stick me in a nursing home? Or a cemetery?" (93).

Despite such deflations, Robert Merriwether emerges as one of Stern's most sympathetic characters. His heroism resides in his openness to love, his refusal to live without it. After the affair is out in the open, Merriwether says to Sarah, "I'm not a cactus. I couldn't endure without intimacy" (9). But Merriwether is also heroic in his desire not to give up his family, especially his children. He cries when he receives the inevitable call from Sarah's lawyer, and he is preposterously, excruciatingly slow to find somewhere else to live. Indeed, he and Sarah are legally divorced for a month before he leaves their home on Acorn Street, and only then because Sarah evicts him. One other appealing element in Merriwether's character is his honesty with himself, his awareness: "he was alert enough to his ploys and disguises; he could feel under his own sincerest moments other selves criticizing his omissions. He detested these simplifications, these posings" (81). Near the end of the novel Cynthia tells him that he is "the best scientific writer in the world," but the narrator lets us know that Merriwether is not really flattered: "This extravagance undercut the praise. More and more, Merriwether relished accuracy" (231).

Two truths emerge from *Other Men's Daughters*. The first is the supreme value of love. In earlier novels, especially *Golk* and *Stitch*, love is viewed as at best a distraction from great achievements, the last refuge of those who are incapable of anything else. This is Golk's opinion (though he concedes that a "very few . . . have a real talent for it" [*Golk*, 50]), as it is Nina Callahan's in *Stitch*. Sarah Merriwether also wonders if her husband's affair is really the final proof of his mediocrity as a scientist. Merriwether himself begins his affair with Cynthia with similar notions. He tells her that "whatever love is, it is not an accomplishment" and that at his age all he is capable of is "a combination of lust and nostalgia" (29). But later he says of Cynthia, "I feel about her the way Galileo did about the telescope. My feelings for her enlarge my feelings for other things" (82). Merriwether is aware that love usually incapacitates, but *Other Men's Daughters* seems to prove that love can also inspire a person to self-knowledge, growth, even great deeds or works of art.

The other truth has to do more specifically with the kind of love that lasts and is ennobling. A relationship of this kind must be one where both partners are equals. The lack of equality in the Merriwether marriage led inevitably to alienation: "We separated emotionally years ago," says Merriwether. "Probably my fault. Without meaning to I dominated her. That was the way of things. *My* schedule, *my* friends, and . . . *my* money" (135). Despite their differences in age and education, Merriwether does not feel this way about Cynthia. "She's at least my equal," he tells a friend (84). He delights in her wit and intelligence as well as her youth and beauty. When they spend a summer in a villa near Nice, old-fashioned Merriwether even agrees, "at times in theory, always in practice, that house chores be shared" (92). Perhaps another secret of a successful relationship is a recognition of its limitations. At the end of *Other Men's Daughters* Merriwether thinks, "Maybe human beings who love each other should only present their best face to each other, saving their miseries for silence, dark and the pillow" (239). Presumably Merriwether and Cynthia will keep separate apartments when they return to Cambridge, just as Stern and Alane Rollings did in the years immediately after Stern's divorce.

After *Other Men's Daughters*

If *Other Men's Daughters* is a culmination, it is also a turning point.
After *Other Men's Daughters* Stern's protagonists still often resemble
their creator, and the ex-wives and girlfriends to varying degrees still
often mirror Stern's ongoing relationships with his ex-wife, Gay
Stern, and girlfriend and later-to-be second wife, Alane Rollings. The
relationships between these characters are, however, never again the
primary center of interest in Stern's fictions. No doubt this shift of
"romantic" material to the background of his fictions reflects the relative stability that Stern has established with both women in the
years since *Other Men's Daughters* was published in 1973. Furthermore, "mirror" is perhaps not the best word to describe the connection between the fictitious and the real relationships. Stern's
renderings are just as likely to be about roads not taken as they are
to be about the actual traveled roads of his life.

Versions of the Stern triad – ex-husband, ex-wife, and girlfriend – appear in each of the three novels Stern has published since
Other Men's Daughters, though there are many variations from book
to book in how each member of the triad is depicted. In *Natural
Shocks* the Stern counterpart is journalist Frederic Wursup, author of
the best-seller *Down the American Drain*, a book about "the disastrous brilliance of recent American leadership" (17). From the roof
of his Manhattan apartment Wursup spies on his ex-wife, Susannah,
and his two teenage sons who live a few blocks away. Wursup's
occasional surveillance is not motivated by jealousy or desire but by
a Prospero-like benevolent regard: "he wished Susannah well; he
cared for her well-being, and he guessed that meant he cared for her
too" (11). During the time of the divorce Wursup saw a "fury" in
Susannah he had not realized existed beneath her temperament of
"amored stupor" (10). Now, three years later, they "were more or
less easy with each other; friendly, if not exactly friends" (11).

Wursup regards Susannah's narrow, Puritanical life of exclusion
with concern. When he sees through his field glasses the empty
spaces on her calendar, he feels anger at their former friends for not
inviting her places; they were "turning her into a No-Person" (14).
Although Wursup can see that Susannah is "stranded in the shallow-
est part of her nature" (204), he does not understand why. One reason, the narrator explains, is guilt about her two-year affair (now

over) with Wursup's editor and best friend, Will Eddy. Wursup, who had been guilty of infidelities of his own, never learns about the betrayal. As the novel progresses, Wursup observes the developing romance between Susannah and Kevin Miyako, the editor of *Chouinard's News Letter*, the small publication where she works. This relationship culminates in marriage.

Cynthia Ryder's successor in *Natural Shocks* is Sookie Gompert, "a mature, a brilliant, woman, a geophysicist who lectured all over the world on what made it tick and rumble, she was a permanent adolescent about her looks" (30). Wursup prefers her natural beauty to the artificial one she spends hours at the mirror each day to create, her "old conviction of ugliness instilled by a thousand sisterly digs and a girlhood of unfavorable comparison to the models in *Mademoiselle, Glamour,* and *Vogue*" (30). This relationship seems in transition, bordered by ambiguities. They keep separate apartments, the arrangement Merriwether favors at the end of *Other Men's Daughters*, yet Sookie spends half her nights at Wursup's. They do not use the word *love* with each other, even though she and Wursup "had spun a thousand marriagelike threads between them" (31); "their amorous creed was *No Chains*," the narrator says, "but something deeper demanded sexual strictness" (70).

Aside from the small drama of Susannah's courtship and marriage, the romantic interest in *Natural Shocks* is restricted to Wursup's relationship with Cicia Buell, a 19-year-old woman who is dying of melanoma. Wursup first meets Cicia in a hospital while he is writing an essay on death for a monthly journal.[5] Wursup is gripped by a "love seizure" for Cicia (90), even feels an "amorous" warmth for her (97). Shaken by his unexpected desire, he wonders if he has become a necrophiliac. "I doubt that," says Will Eddy. "Isn't it the oldest feeling in the world? Loving what's not going to be around. The deepest feeling, anyway. You're no different from anyone else" (124). Unlike Wursup's relationships with Susannah and Sookie, which are clearly based on Stern's with Gay Stern and Alane Rollings, the relationship with Cicia does not seem to have an autobiographical source.[6]

In *A Father's Words* first-person narrator/protagonist Cyrus Riemer is the editor of a scientific newsletter. He is on fairly good terms with his ex-wife, Agnes, author of the children's book *Arthur the Anteater* and the mother of his four children. In this fictional

incarnation of Stern's first marriage and divorce, the ex-husband is
guilty of adultery, not the ex-wife. Perhaps this is why Cy agreed not
to get his own attorney and quietly listened to the "caricature" of
himself "drawn from Agnes's discontent" by her lawyer Kraypoole
(18). Agnes, Cy tells us, "is boring beyond toleration"; he had called
her – and the children heard – "Mrs. Tedium Vitae" (18), although
he also says that she is "admirable, decent, good-looking" (19).
When he helps her pack for her trip to Africa and the Peace Corps,
he tries to allay her fears about traveling and even feels a resurgence
of love for her: "I feared for Agnes, this good person whom I'd
wronged and been wronged by, whom I'd loved and, in a scarcely
noticed part of myself, apparently still loved. (Was – in a way – still
true to and about. I wanted to hear nothing against her, and remembered nothing of the many bad times we'd had)" (129). It has been
Agnes who has held the family together; her departure for Africa pre-
cipitates change in Cy's relations with his four children.

Cy's girlfriend in *A Father's Words* is Emma, who is less secure
and less professionally accomplished than Sookie Gompert in *Natural Shocks* but no less loved by Cy than Sookie is by Wursup. Cy
describes Emma as being "wonderful . . . delightful, loyal, full of
love, funnier than the funniest comics, intelligent in fifty ways, as
pure in heart as people can be," but he adds, "there is also the
Emma of self-hatred, hysteria, and despair. Self-hatred rotates with
hatred of others, including me. Especially me. For as I am – she
says – everything to her, I must be what she can hate as well as love"
(30). Emma feels excluded from "the Riemersphere" (22), especially
when she is not invited to the wedding of Cy's son Jack. She wants
the validation of marriage. She wants a child, and when Cy resists,
she equates his irresponsibility with Jack's: "He's like you. Won't
commit himself," she complains (29). To her demand for a child, Cy
says that his fathering is over, that he has done his "seminal job"
(30). He already has four children, handful enough. And he thinks of
Emma very often as a fifth child, especially during one of her depressions during which she reverts to the personality of a five-year-old.

Perhaps this is the significance of the role reversals and the
affectionate babytalk ("that pornography of lovers" [28]) Riemer and
Emma speak to each other: he becomes "Fay," while she becomes
"Kong." Cy is her child as much as she is his, and his reluctance to
father another child may also conceal a desire not to share Emma,

even with his own child. "I like no one more than you" (120),
Riemer tells her when she feels jealous of Cy's children. The novel
concludes with Cy married to Emma, with Emma pregnant with Cy's
child (181). Though they have no children, Stern and Alane Rollings
did marry in 1985, the year before *A Father's Words* was published.

George and Robert Share, the two protagonists of Stern's novel
Shares, have different professions and live in different worlds from
each other and from their author. George Share is a college drop-
out, an autodidact, and the owner of a very successful shoe store in
fictitious Willsville, Illinois. George is also a one-man beacon of culture, the "Shoe Store Plato" (*Shares*, 114). His Share Complex – "six
rooms of George's nine-room house" – is the "only place within a
couple of hundred miles where the world's best old movies can be
seen, where there is a complete file of the *New York Review of
Books*, a twenty-year file of the *Hudson* and *Partisan Reviews*, *Arts
News*, *Paris Match* and *Der Spiegel*" (113). Brother Robert Share is a
deputy secretary of state who has risen to this position of power and
prominence via the University of Iowa, the University of Chicago Law
School, and a Wall Street firm. Despite such professional differences
from Stern, it is possible to see George and Robert as a bifurcated
self-portrait.

Robert Share is linked to earlier Stern-like protagonists, especially Cyrus Riemer, by the problems he has had and continues to
have with his children, especially his now middle-aged son, Reg.
Unlike Riemer, however, Robert is still happily married after "four
decades of intimacy" to Eileen (130), the mother of his children. The
Robert-Eileen marriage resembles husband-wife relationships in
recent stories like "In Return" and "The Illegibility of the World."
Perhaps these harmonious couples represent Stern's imaginary
merging of the best aspects of his relationships with his two wives.
Like Gay Stern, these female characters share with the Stern protagonist a love of and concern about the children. Like Alane Rollings,
these fictitious wives enjoy long-term, loving, mutually supportive
relationships with their husbands.

What bachelor George shares with his Sternian precursors is a
love of younger women. George's own quarters within the Share
Complex "are convenient and private enough to give confidence to
the young women who over the years moved from the deep chairs of
the Complex to George's kitchen, bath and living room-bedroom"

(114). Through his "Share Fellowship," George has managed to live discreetly for six or seven weeks in Europe with a different young woman each year. Occasionally, there have been threats of scandal, but George's wise gifts to local charities have "blunted criticism" (135), and he has tried to be discreet: "he gave 'the Share Fellows' tickets to Chicago and they went there by themselves; he followed; and the girls were sworn to silence" (135). At 55, George has found getting young women to travel with him and share his bed increasingly difficult ("It went more slowly, heavily and fearfully than ever" [139]), and as the novel opens, George is almost ready to throw in the erotic towel. But then he sees 20-year-old Junebug Venerdy, the daughter of Alicia, who was his Share Companion 22 years earlier. Alicia trusts that George would have more decency than to ask her daughter to become a Share Fellow ("It was Sodom and Gomorrah," she thinks [139]). All George can think of is his "ache of need" for Bug (139). To his surprise and great pleasure, Bug agrees to accompany him to Venice; "Alicia said nothing" (140).

The age difference between George and Bug is 35 years. Perhaps their relationship is an exaggerated version – or even a parody – of Cynthia and Merriwether, and therefore of Alane Rollings and Stern. The artist Frothingham's comment when he sees Bug with Reg Share has an edge of satire: "Hey there, pretty one. Dumped the old gent, have you?" (168). While George cools himself in a bathtub filled with ice cubes, exhausted from the heat, Bug shows Venice – and herself – to Reg. The fact that George is cuckolded by his nephew (in a sense, his son) also makes the fantasy rich in Oedipal complexity as well as autobiographical resonances.

Of course, it is foolish to imagine too exact a correspondence between characters in these stories and novels and important people (including Stern) in Stern's life. There are too many versions of each member of the triad in too many fictions for any one version to gain the status of "true portrait." One ex-wife is short and stocky, another tall and thin. One girlfriend is a blonde, another a brunette. Susannah Wursup marries a second time. Gay Stern has not remarried. Sarah Merriwether is frigid; Susannah Wursup is guilty of 500 acts of adultery. At the end of *A Father's Words* Emma gives birth to a child; Alane Rollings and Richard Stern have no children. Bug Venerdy has as much in common with the nonautobiographical Cicia Buell in

Natural Shocks as she does with Cynthia, Sookie, or Emma, all based to some degree on Alane Rollings.

Despite such differences among characters, there can be no denying the many resemblances to real people scattered through Stern's fiction. For those with some knowledge of Stern's life and work, such resemblances clearly provide an added level of interest. It is doubtful that Stern is deliberately playing on this interest, depending on a local shock effect to add power and appeal to his fiction. More likely, he is working through relationships, coming to understand them and himself better, shedding selves and obsessions through the act of re-creating them in fiction. Thus, in a 1978 interview, Stern said he sometimes consoles himself with "the notion that one doesn't have a given self upon which one preys. One's always becoming. So that each fiction represents a special exertion of self-creation. One has made a child out of one's old self" (Birtwistle, 186).

Whether Stern's ex-wife, current wife, children, and friends take heart from such consolations remains to be seen. They are not always likely to appreciate the ways they are represented. Stern might well appeal to the benefits of psychological release, the love of truth and honesty, the high purpose of art, and literary license; close family and friends might tell – and in Stern's fiction, sometimes do tell – a different story.

Chapter Eight

Fatherhood

I said to Emma, "Sometimes I feel I'm nothing but my bonds." (Meaning, that's why I don't want any more.) "Just a depot of connections." (Cyrus Riemer, *A Father's Words*, 71)

A father of four children, Richard Stern often explores in his fiction the relationships between fathers and their sons and daughters. In his foreword to the 1987 Phoenix edition of *Golk*, Bernard Rodgers, Jr., writes, "Where Philip Roth's heroes are, above all, sons, where Saul Bellow's are, above all, ex-husbands, Stern's are most often and most importantly fathers. Like John Updike's or John Irving's, his novels are full of a parent's heartrending doubts and fears, a father's sometimes inarticulate but always profound feelings toward his children" (x). Rodgers's contention about fatherhood in Stern's fiction is certainly valid for many of the autobiographical stories and novels – works that Stern, in fact, has referred to as "family novels" (*PB*, 180). But even before Richard Stern started writing fictional versions of his own life and relationships, the complexity of fatherhood is often an important theme for him.

In a few of the early works the depiction of fathers and children is decidedly unsentimental. "Arrangements at the Gulf," for example, presents protagonist Fred Lomax, who asks his close friend Herbert Granville to be with him in Florida when he – Lomax – dies. Lomax prefers the company of his friend to that of his children and grandchildren: "There were twenty people at the station to see me off, and, except for three in-laws, not one of them would have been alive except for me. But that's all, Granville. Could have been any twenty people in the station, any twenty off the Chicago gutters, and they would have been as near to me as those. As near and as understanding. The virtue of children is the fiction of bachelors" (*NR*, 257). For Lomax, "true family" are "old friends" (258).

Our first view of Max Schreiber in *Europe: Or Up or Down with Baggish and Schreiber* is through the eyes of his young daughter, Valerie, who despises him. Six years earlier, when she was seven, her life was disturbed "by the fat slob who had one day invaded their lives in his captain's uniform, and then, doffing it, had played the other oh-so-cute game of being her father" (3). When, a chapter later, Schreiber leaves his family and lawyer's practice and goes to Europe, he does so without much thought about abandoning either his wife or his daughter. And once in Europe, he is reported thinking of Valerie only once, though on that occasion he thinks of her with "a rich sense of guilt" that, "soaked in wine and joined with other pleasures of the evening, made him dissolve with melancholy pleasure" (86).

Bonds of Love

The theme of fatherhood in *Golk* is more complex and more developed than in *Europe*. It is also based to some degree on Stern's relationship with his father, but even more, Stern says it is inspired by his father's relationship with *his* father ("On *Golk*," 32; see also: Appendix). Poppa Hondorp, the ear-nose-and-throat doctor, is loving but overly possessive. When his 37-year-old son gets his first job, joining Golk's "You're on Camera" crew, the old man is threatened and hurt. On one occasion right after he begins working, Hondorp arrives home late (he has been having sex with Elaine) to find his father staring blankly into the television set. When Hondorp asks if his father is still awake, the old man "simultaneously whack[s] . . . both cheeks" and then pronounces that no son of his "is coming home at four o'clock in the morning." But right after the pronouncement the father "burst into tears, kissed the cheeks where he'd slapped them, and waddled off down the hall to his bedroom" (69). After this episode Poppa Hondorp does his best to suppress his sense of injury at his son's independence; the result of his stoicism is that a lipoma begins to form around the base of his neck.

One morning as he arrives at work Hondorp is shocked to see that his father has become Golk's latest victim on film. Golk, posing as a patient with an ear problem, lures Poppa Hondorp onto the subject of fatherhood:

"Father and son," said Golk, as if inscribing a chapter heading on a blank manuscript.

Poppa Hondorp filled in the page. "A noble relationship. But packed to the margins, packed, impacted with heartbreak. With great heartbreak." He went to the window, his lipoma pointing angrily askew like an auxiliary, but mutinous head.

"Ingratitude, the serpent's tooth," urged Golk wistfully.

Poppa Hondorp's lipoma swayed in what seemed negation. "That's too strong," he said. "The matter is not treason, just – how shall I say it? – a carelessness, inattention, lack of thought, but terrible, all terrible. Worse might be better. You would be stiffened to resist. But against so soft a thing, who can push?" (75-76)

Hondorp's Oedipal "thrust" to independence (Stern uses the word *patricidal* [28]) is brought about by his success as a member of Golk's crew. By the time Hondorp and Hendricks take over the show Hondorp rarely visits his father. And when Poppa Hondorp dies Hondorp either forgets to tell – or chooses not to tell – Hendricks. For her this is the ultimate proof of Hondorp's dehumanization. Ironically, Golk's *King Lear* paraphrase ("Ingratitude, the serpent's tooth") turns out to be a prophecy of his own relationship with Hondorp, for Golk becomes Hondorp's surrogate father, and true to form, Hondorp, the son, betrays him.

The Chaleur Network offers a very different kind of father-son relationship. For one thing, this novel presents the father's point of view rather than the son's. Samuel Curry's mourning for his son is complicated by guilt. During Bobbie's childhood, especially after the boy's mother died, Curry's love for the boy was often in competition with his pursuit of available women. Not that Curry was always unkind to his son; after an angry, sometimes even brutal reprimand (perhaps Bobbie had disturbed his love-making or awakened him when he was hung over), Curry would overcompensate with affectionate, sorrowful, midnight apologies: "'You lousy brute,' I'd tell myself, 'how can you abuse that motherless boy who's got only you in this world?' and I'd go down the long hall to his room, sit on his bed and take his little blacktop head in my arms" (2). On one occasion, when Bobbie was still a boy, he called a foot fault on his father during a tennis match between Curry and a friend. The next instant Curry flung his racket at Bobbie's head; the racket missed and got caught in a tree. When Curry approached with the wooden press to dislodge the racket Bobbie feared his father was going to hit him.

Curry states, "My insides somersaulted. I dropped the press, ran over, put my arms around him and apologized over and over while the blossoms came down on our heads" (81).

Once Bobbie had grown to manhood Curry scarcely knew him. Nevertheless, when he reads the accusation of treason against Bobbie in Father Trentemille's book, Curry is certain of his son's innocence and honor. This conviction about Bobbie's character motivates Curry to discover the truth. In rescuing Bobbie's reputation Curry redeems himself. Having completed his mission, Curry says he has "come closer to being what fathers are supposed to be." He has "staked" more of himself than ever before and ends up "somewhat more than when [he] started." Then he adds, "I feel with Bobbie a blood kinship of change and testing, brother as much as father to him, and perhaps his son as well" (233).

Richard Stern began writing about his own experiences as a father at roughly the same time that his real-life marital problems were finding their way into his fiction – that is, around the time he was writing *Stitch*. And just as he makes some effort to disguise himself and his wife in these depictions, so too does he frequently alter the sexes, ages, and ordering of his children. In fact, of all his works only *Veni, Vidi . . . Wendt* has the children in the "right" order, with the "right" ages and sexes.[1] Initially, these autobiographical fictions of fatherhood are presented within the larger context of a disintegrating marriage; the fear of losing the children, the pain of separation from them, is an important pressure on the hearts and minds of Stern's male protagonists who struggle in the marital net.

In *Stitch*, for example, Edward Gunther says farewell to his youngest child, Quentin, before setting out from Venice on an adulterous tour of Bologna and Rome with a young American woman, Sibyl: "Quent stumbled toward Edward, who ran out to scoop up the dearest twenty pounds of his life, put his own shaven cheek next to the sweet softness of the baby's, kissed his eyes, ears, and – discarding sanitary fears, pushing down the mouth-high muffler – the tiny, full, damp lips. Like kissing a soul. . . . What adoration he felt. It was an awful wrench, departing even for a day, going God knows how far from children's accidents" (143-44). Later, after the inevitable separation from Cressida, Edward suffers in California because he almost cannot bear the pain of being apart from his children. When Cressida refuses to have him back, he contemplates sui-

cide but finds he lacks the courage and will to surrender: "His children, his beloved, precious children. What would they be told?
Daddy would not be coming quite yet. He was sick. Next month. No,
the summer, and then, visits. Yes, there would be those. . . . Quentin.
If he had a gun. If he had courage. If the water weren't so cold. If he
could keep even miserable long enough" (204).

Robert Merriwether's paternal agonies in *Other Men's Daughters*
are, if anything, more poignantly rendered than Gunther's. When he
returns from his summer in Nice with Cynthia he decides he must tell
his oldest two children, Albie and Priscilla, what has happened (as
he suspects, they have seen the article in *Newsweek* that mentions
Cynthia). With both children, he begins by telling them that they
have been – are – "the most important things in [his] life" (142), but
to his son he adds, "but there was a big empty place there too. Now
someone's there" (134). Later, when he tells his younger daughter,
Esmé, about the divorce some six weeks after the fact, Merriwether
feels "a depth of love absolutely new in his life" (220). And two
weeks after he tells his youngest child, George, about the divorce:
"the thought came to Merriwether that the moments holding each
other on the bed were the best he and George would probably have
together; it was as strong a love as two human beings could have for
each other without sexuality (stronger for its absence)" (221).

Of course, some readers might ask, If Stern's protagonists love
their children so intensely, why do they not deny themselves their
girlfriends and try to patch up their marriages? Stern does not avoid
the question; instead, he continually invites it. And his answer seems
obvious: marriages like those of the Gunthers, Wendts, and Merriwethers are beyond repair. The choices are thus those of separation
or survival in relationships without love. Some of the protagonists,
like Wendt, do stay married, though they manage to do so only by
being unfaithful. To live without sexual intimacy is too great a sacri-
fice for Stern's needy, discontented men; the love of the children,
the satisfaction of being with them, is not for them a sufficient substi-
tute for romantic, sexual love, much less for real communion with
another adult.

People can make such sacrifices for their children – they do so
all the time – but Stern's male protagonists, at least those removed
from unhappy marriages, would say such people are living half-lives.
And Stern's unhappy women would grumble their agreement. Cres-

sida Gunther *chooses* to separate from Edward. When Sarah Merriwether forces Robert out of the house, she reminds herself that she
cannot tolerate his presence, not even for the sake of the children:
"Not for the children. No, she'd lived so much for children, and
happily, but she was not going to die for them" (*OMD*, 139-40). In
Stern's fiction, as in life, children suffer from a bad marriage as much
as their parents. "You two better get a divorce if you have to argue,"
says young George Merriwether when he hears his parents bickering
again (146). Moments later Merriwether wonders, "What in this
world was worth bringing misery to this precious person?" (146).

Occasionally this paternal love threatens to take more destructive forms. Some parents presume to get *too close* to their children.
Merriwether and Albie in *Other Men's Daughters* illustrate a pattern
found in other Stern fictions: the father who shares intimate, disturbing, or embarrassing secrets with his son, as though the son
were the father's equal in age and experience or shared the father's
values. The son usually feels uncomfortable with the burden of such
confidences. When Merriwether tries to justify to Albie his affair with
Cynthia, Albie is anxious to change the subject: he "had had as much
of his father's confession as he could take. He did not want to hear
any more" (135).

A similar situation occurs in "Gifts," a story first published in
1968. Protagonist Williams's "only confidant" is his 18-year-old son
(*NR*, 114). Williams describes for him a recent trip to Mexico and an
affair with a young Indian woman whom Williams hired as his guide.
At Uxmal Williams and the girl climbed the steep stairs of the gover-
nor's palace. At the top they began to struggle: "I grabbed at her
arms, we pulled and wrestled around, sex in it, but fight too" (119).
Suddenly, the girl fell, rolling down 20 stone steps. Williams tells his
son that he rushed to her side, found her unconscious, and in a
panic abandoned her (he later sent a doctor and left pesos for her at
the hotel). The son, clearly repulsed by his father's behavior, advises
him to call the hotel in Mexico to see if the young woman is all right
(it turns out that "she'd only broken her arm" [120]). "It was," the
narrator states, "the last advice he was going to give his father. And,
if he could manage it, he had heard the man's last confession" (120).

Another cloud that darkens the paternal horizon is the threat of
incestuous desire fathers in Stern's fiction might feel for their daughters, though this desire is in almost every instance flatly denied or

displaced onto other girls. "I'm sure I never had an incestuous thought in my life," says Cyrus Riemer, who in a sense speaks for all Stern's fathers of daughters, but then Riemer adds, "though I grant this assurance may be the freeze laid on the wildness beneath" (*FW*, 179). Many of Stern's preautobiographical protagonists show a penchant for younger women. Thirty-seven-year-old Hondorp, for example, enjoys the favors of Elaine and Hendricks, both in their twenties, and Samuel Curry has an affair with and marries Jacqueline, who is more than twenty years his junior. Jacqueline is also the woman who probably would have become his daughter-in-law if Bobbie had lived. The pattern of older men and younger women – as well as the incest motif – is thus present in Stern's fiction before it was likely to have been autobiographical.

The protagonist of *Veni, Vidi . . . Wendt* is not aware of any sexual desire in himself for his teenage daughter, Gina; instead Wendt lusts for his bikini-clad teenage niece, Mina, whose "Northwest Passage" Wendt dreams of opening: "Mina is Jeff-U's age. Two strips of psychedelic cloth hang on five and a half feet of intoxicating flesh. Her vitaminized breasts are those of Hungarian spies; her golden triangle – how I imagine its secretive fur – her pure, thick lips, her winking invitations to the ball I think are meant for me. I have seen her beauty spill over since sixty-four. Even then, she was ready, lolitable. (We watched that film together on the late show. How she understood)" (*Shares*, 49).

The allusion to Nabokov is appropriate; the similarity in the names Mina and Gina is just the sort of play Nabokov loved. The transference of incestuous desire reaches an ironic anticlimax later in the novella when Wendt goes for a midnight swim, sans bathing trunks, with the hope that another young woman, a 19-year-old neighbor, will join him in the water. While he waits, he recalls a story in his son's *Playboy* about a " 'mild-mannered man' who'd had relations with seventeen members of his immediate family, including father and grandmother" (101). When Wendt, already in the water, sees a woman approach, he calls out to her in the dark, but instead of his seductive neighbor, his daughter answers instead. "Something in the region of my heart," Wendt says, "dives through something like my intestines, slaps my bare gonads, sinks in my bowels" (101). The embarrassed father asks his daughter to throw him his trunks.

Also in *1968* is the story "Gaps," which features the newly wid-owed William McCoshan (his wife, Elsie, died in a car accident six months earlier). A travel agent who has never traveled, McCoshan takes his teenage daughter, Winnie, on a three-week European vaca-tion even though "she was not his type." In Rome, however, Winnie meets her closest friend's boyfriend, Robert, and, "with the flirta-tious power of adolescent treason," decides to stay with him (*NR*, 50). McCoshan, therefore, sets out on his own for France, picks up a hitchhiker, a 16-year-old Flemish girl whom he deflowers on a deserted beach. The story ends with McCoshan's early, unexpected, and unwelcomed return to Winnie and Robert in Rome. Winnie "raises her face painfully for a kiss. William cannot put his lips there. He smells an unscheduled knowledge" (59). One of the gaps in "Gaps," clearly, is the one between McCoshan's feelings for his daughter and his actions with the Flemish girl.

In the novels *Other Men's Daughters*, *Natural Shocks*, and *A Father's Words* the pattern of older male protagonist and younger girlfriend reflects Stern's relationship with Alane Rollings. Yet even in these works there is the occasional suggestion of incestuous desire. The closeness in age between Cynthia Ryder and his daughter Priscilla does not escape Robert Merriwether (or Cynthia) in *Other Men's Daughters*. Indeed, the title of this novel hints at the idea of incest. Yet when Merriwether thinks of his daughter's beauty he is appropriately subdued in his thoughts: "He assumed a lovely body, he had not seen her nude for ten years, had no desire to, remained New England where it counted, in distance, privacy, the sacred space of one's own body, every person's zone of repose" (33). Still, it is more than coincidence that Merriwether and Cynthia first lie down together in oldest daughter Priscilla's room, on Priscilla's bed. And it is equally significant that Merriwether leaves the sleeping Cynthia without making love with her and returns to his marriage bed (where the next morning he and Cynthia do make love). It is as if Cynthia symbolically passes from the role of daughter to that of mistress/wife. Even after this rite of passage, however, Cynthia is not beyond reminding Merriwether (as if he needed a reminder) of how perilous a passage it has been. In France she teases him by reading a letter she pretends to write to his daughter:

"Dear Priscilla, Hi. You don't know me, but your name was given to me by a mutual acquaintance. He said we have much in common. We are both in college. I like college. Do you like college? Are you lonely? I am! I only have one good friend. Are you a virgin? I am not. Your loving stepmother, Cynthia Ryder." (104)

In a similar vein, Cynthia later suggests that she and Merriwether introduce her father to Priscilla. Merriwether "drove on the wrong side of the road until she said she was sorry" (123).

In *Natural Shocks* protagonist Frederick Wursup has close relationships with two younger women, his geologist girlfriend Sookie Gompert and Cicia Buell, but in *Natural Shocks* there are no intimations of the incest taboo since Wursup has no daughters, only two college-age sons. *A Father's Words*, however, does offer further insight into the older man – younger woman / father – daughter nexus in Stern's work. Cyrus Riemer's girlfriend, Emma, wants to get married and have children, but Riemer resists because in many ways Emma is like a fifth child, especially when she is depressed. In *Shares* George Share takes a different young woman to Europe each summer. Each year the age difference increases, and the sexual negotiations become more awkward and arduous. When he chooses Bug Venerdy as his Share Companion he chooses the daughter of Alicia Venerdy, who was herself a Share Companion 22 years earlier. George is old enough to be Bug's father, even her grandfather. Since he was her mother's lover two decades earlier, the remote possibility that Share *is* Bug's father comes to mind (though Stern never mentions it directly and would probably think the idea far-fetched).

The Laius Complex

For the male children, particularly the eldest male children, Stern's fathers' love is often mingled with contention. This rivalry between father and son – because it is usually viewed in Stern's fiction from the father's point of view – might best be called the "Laius Complex." At least this is what Emma calls Cyrus Riemer's obsession with his eldest son, Jack, in *A Father's Words*. "You've got all those feelings – whatever they are – the reverse of the Oedipal ones. The Laius complex," she says (24). Symptoms include the father's fear of being toppled, supplanted, or even rivaled by the son. Sometimes the love of the wife/mother or girlfriend is at stake. Often the father's fortunes seem to bear an inverse relation to the son's. If the father prospers, the son usually does not. Those sons in Stern's fiction who do prosper often thrive at the father's expense. Consequently, the father's fear can result in the repression/symbolic emasculation of the child, the destruction of his defenses. The complex, for obvious reasons, causes the father enormous guilt if and when the son fails to mature properly.[2]

The symptoms can be seen in Poppa Hondorp's attempts to repress his son's sudden (and belated) independence in *Golk* as well as in Poppa Hondorp's decline when the younger Hondorp appears to succeed. The complex can also be seen throughout the presumably nonautobiographical novel *The Chaleur Network* (though, interestingly, the book is dedicated to Stern's eldest son, Christopher, who in 1962 was 11). When Bobbie was "about three," Curry recalls, the boy would often wake in the night with a bad dream and climb into his mother's bed. Once Curry returned to his room from the lavatory "and got in on the other side of Hélène and held on to her, held on to her being alive by the little beats of her stomach and heart. And then [he] felt Bobbie's round little hand holding on also, two sailors on a life raft, and [he, Curry] got out and went back down the hall free of all but the sediment of fear, uncertainty and relief" (116). Earlier in the novel Curry describes an Atlantic crossing with Bobbie (at this point an adolescent) that was marred by their competition for the same girl. In fact, during their three months in the States "rivalry infected" everything they did (69).

Even Curry's "selfless mission" to clear Bobbie's name runs into Laiusian complications. When Curry investigates the Chaleur Network, he meets and falls in love with Jacqueline, a former member of the network and his son's former lover. (In fairness to Curry, he is attracted to her before he realizes her former relationship with his son.) As Curry becomes more deeply involved with Jacqueline, he finds himself locked in rivalry with the memory of his dead son. After making love with her for the first time, for example, Curry imagines "Bobbie . . . sending down the judgement" (157), and not long after he hears a voice (actually, a pointing "Eye-Finger") accusing him, "Curry, you Curry, you and your own son, you and he have had this war of love. Where you should have helped each other through the

world, you've tripped over each other's footsteps. It was not
intended by nature, law, custom" (159).

In *Stitch* the sentimental father Gunther has problems with
Brose, his eldest son: they "were equally competitive, and
though they had drawn closer together in their European isolation
than they'd ever been – for the first time Edward regarded the
eleven-year-old boy as a friend to whom he sometimes spilled his latest insights into world affairs and doubts about his own – there was
an active baiting of each other which frequently culminated
in arguments, shouting, accusation, and blows" (51-52). After losing
to Brose and daughter Cammie at blackjack, Edward shouts the children out of his room, then moments later, when he hears Brose brag
to his mother about winning, Edward angrily spanks the boy. The
following day the repentant father apologizes and gives each child
1,000 lire (53).

Relations between father and eldest son are also conflicted in
Veni, Vidi . . . Wendt. Composer Jeffrey Wendt is usually critical of
his namesake, 17-year-old Jeff-U. For example, he faults the teenager
for watching too much television when he should be reading Dos-
toyevski's *The Possessed*. "Rage and disdain," we are told, "darken
his [Jeff-U's] long face" (*Shares*, 58). Moments later the father gives
the reader a portrait of his son: "A dear boy, wiser than his savage
pa, and no power-mad know-it-all, no instant-revolutionary, pimpled
Robespierre shrieker, no louse-ridden Speed-lapper, hardly a drinker
. . . not even a bad driver. Only vanity, sloth, and narcissism blot
him" (58). The day after Jeff-U beats his father on the tennis court
for the second day in a row (the tennis court is the site of furious
father-son battles in other works by Stern as well) Wendt gets into a
squabble with Jeff-U about changing the sheets on the guest bed and
cleaning sand from the bathtub. When the son resists, Wendt bears
down harder. When Jeff-U says "Eff-U" the angry father shoves him
and even punches his arm, "hard" (68-69). The frightened boy cries
out for his mother, and Wendt, startled by the depth of his own
anger, feels "disgust at [his] violent failure as a father" (69). The
novella ends in tenderness, back in Chicago, the week before Jeff-U
goes off to college, with the father giving his son a back rub and
affectionately recalling to himself scenes from Jeff-U's infancy and
childhood.

Though warm feelings toward the children predominate in *Other Men's Daughters*, there is still room for criticism when Merriwether discovers that Albie, his eldest son, has been writing term papers for profit – a job Merriwether tries to persuade him to quit. "I don't feel much like an example these days, Albie," he says, "and I don't want to impose my standards on you, but I feel this is so direct a repudiation of my life, I have to say something" (180). Later, writing a check to Albie so that the boy cannot use money as his excuse for the dishonorable job, Merriwether wonders if "Albie's choice could have something to do with the invisible poison of the household. Underneath the civility, Albie had suffered the decay; and now he was attacking another part of the moral structure" (181). Merriwether is a typical Stern father in both his harsh judgment of his son and in his internalization of his son's guilt.

This mixture of criticism of and guilt toward the eldest son becomes a major interest in *A Father's Words*, Stern's treatise on fatherhood, a book that distills the joys and agonies, the blindness and insight, of all Stern's flawed but loving fathers. Cyrus Riemer and ex-wife Agnes have survived a divorce and have reestablished amicable relations, and Cy has never lost contact with his grown children. In some ways, in fact, he is too involved in their lives, and lately he senses signs of some resentment of him. His youngest child, Livy, is an FBI agent who complains that Cy knows "more about Darwin and Rilke" than he knows about himself (15). In return, Cy worries about Livy being unmarried and fears that his "daughter's life was moving from A.M. to P.M. before she knew it" (162). Ben and Jenny (Jenny is the eldest child) have each written books critical of family life: Ben's is titled *The Need to Hurt* ("the first fetal history of mankind" [17]), while Jenny's doctoral dissertation is "The Wobbling Nucleus: The Family in Literature from *Medea* to *Finnegans Wake*." Cy worries also that Jenny's reluctance to have children (she's married to a career diplomat) reflects some "barrenness" in her that is a silent rebuke to him. Ben at least gets his wife pregnant during the novel.

Most of Cy's worry, however, is reserved for his second child and eldest son, Jack. In his thirties, still without gainful employment (he has had an almost endless string of ill-fated jobs), living off former girlfriends and the occasional parental check, Jack produces in his father a volatile mixture of guilt, fear, pity, anger, and exasperation. When Cy looks at Jack he sees "only broken promises" and

wasted potential, and Cy worries that he is to blame, perhaps
because of the divorce or because of his obvious disapproval of his
son (21). The novel traces several of Jack's misadventures (e.g., his
brief job on the Commodities Exchange; his marriage to and separation from Maria Robusto, daughter of a notorious pornographer)
and Cy's parental despair. Early in the narrative Cy receives a letter
from a woman who let Jack stay in her apartment. She returns to find
excrement smeared on her walls and a $942 phone bill. Cy is morti-
fied. "All I know," he explains to Emma, "is I can't tolerate the way
he acts and looks. After all, he's mine. I helped shape him. His life's a
rebuke to mine. And since I know his laziness and hypocrisy are
mine, too, it makes it worse. The difference is *I* try to squeeze that
stuff out of me. I don't think Jack tries" (24).

The portrayal of the relationship is more balanced than one
might suppose, given the father as the first-person narrator. For one
thing, Stern gives Cy definite weaknesses. Thus Emma says, "Even
Livy says you're less in touch with your unconscious than anyone
she knows" (119). For another thing, Stern reports what Jack says
about how he feels (mainly misunderstood), and after a particularly
bad quarrel between Jack and Cy, eldest daughter Jenny shows up at
her father's apartment, furious on her brother's behalf. Cy had inti-
mated that Jack's indolence and irresponsibility might lead him to a
criminal career and eventually to prison (Cy can imagine Jack as a
lawbreaker, but not as a successful one). Jenny accuses Cy of being
unable to stand equality with those around him (which, she says, is
why he chose Emma) and of bullying Jack since he was a child (139).
She deplores in her father "the destructiveness that's there with the
generosity and love" (140). This is the closest Cy has ever come to
quarrelling with Jenny.

The climactic episode occurs near the end of the novel. With
Agnes in the Peace Corps in Africa and after a false alarm with cancer, Cy sets out on a marathon journey to three cities to see each of
his children: St. Louis to visit Livy, Washington to see Ben and Jenny,
and finally New York to see Jack. Cy takes him to lunch at an Italian
restaurant on Amsterdam Avenue, and Stern creates one of his best
meal scenes (there are several in his fiction), a masterpiece of pathos
and humor. Jack, in "baseball cap, T-shirt, and torn denims" orders
"a dozen *moules*, a lobster bisque, filet mignon, a big salad" and "a
forty-dollar bottle of Bordeaux" (167). The father watches his son

"eat and drink with that semioblivious rapture you see in animals, lost in what they're transforming into themselves" (167). Jack mentions a television project he is working on without contract but says that all he wants to do in life is study philosophy: "Old-line philosophy. The big questions. They're so deceptive, they seem so easy" (169). Cy is not reassured by such plans; outside the restaurant he suggests that Jack "talk with a professional, a therapist of some sort" (172). When Jack more or less refuses, Riemer offers him money, $2,000 and then some to pay his overdue rent, to tide him over until his television contract comes through. Jack stops in the street, Broadway, and responds, "Face it, Dad. I'm finished. I'm never going to be what you want me to be. You can't buy it for me. I can't get it my own way either. Whether you meant it – however you meant it, I appreciate it. But it's beside the point. We missed the train" (174).

Only when Riemer lets go does Jack begin to prosper; in fact his "turnabout . . . had apparently begun . . . the very day of his Declaration of Nullity" (182). Furthermore, Jack succeeds at his father's expense. The pilot to his television show features an "Addled Intellectual whose misapprehension of the world triggers the trouble which his son, the detective, resolves" (183). The father is a "strong-looking man, that is, till his son reveals the selfishness, vanity, and resentment of his son – which drive him" (184). Cy recognizes the distorted portrait of himself (Jack apparently does not until Cy points it out) and dislikes what he sees, but he tells Jack that he enjoyed the show. Cy can take it, or at least he says he can. Besides, Cy has other things to occupy his mind – his "worry quota was filled by George [the name he and Emma give to their new child] and by the parental strikes against [him]: anxieties of age, money, and [his] capacity to handle anxiety itself" (189).

Shares and Other Fictions offers several father-son relationships that resemble the autobiographical pattern found in *A Father's Words* and earlier works. In "The Illegibility of the World," for example, protagonist Larry Biel worries about his son, Peter. Married for a year 10 years ago and then divorced, Peter sells polyvinyl traffic cones for a living and has just changed apartments for the third time in the last five years. In his father's eyes, Peter is in his critical decade and is not doing very well. After playing tennis together, the father watches his son undress; Biel is shocked to see Peter naked: "This man, who as a boy looked like an angel, is into middle age. I look away. I don't want to see him this way" (*Shares*, 9). In therapy to discover if he is even capable of loving, Peter gives his father a copy of Kafka's "The Metamorphosis" to read. The short story makes Biel wonder what is "askew" in his boy, what makes him feel "inadequate, repulsive" (11).

In "The Degradation of Tenderness" and *Shares* Stern uses fiction (or perhaps *fantasy* is a better word) to take the Laius complex to its logical conclusion – the destruction of the father. In "Degradation" psychiatrist Charlie Grasmuck publishes "case studies" of his daughter and son, Patricia and Alfred. Charlie's "arm, his boast, was candor" (*Shares*, 28). Thus he writes of Patricia that her book about a malpractice case against him is really "an act of parricide" in which "devotion and revenge are fused" (28). The portrait of Alfred, the first-person narrator tells us, is much more devastating: "Alfred's defenses, crutches, props and poses were exhibited not only in the name of truth, but love! Charlie didn't miss an Alfredan trick" (29-30). What Charlie does miss is how his children will react to being "dismantled" in print, and this oversight is Charlie's undoing.

Alfred and his new girlfriend, Porphyria Ostreiker ("voluptuousness in Nazi deco," "a minor public menace" [33, 34]), wage "their mad little campaign" against Charlie (34). They picket his office and declare that he is unfit to practice psychiatry. Charlie's practice declines, and not long after he becomes ill with pneumonia, recovers, then loses the will to live and dies because his practice is barren and his children have turned against him. Alfred and Patricia attend the funeral, "heavy with the guilt of those who have had a terrible wish granted" (37). Not long after Alfred dies of Guillaume-Barre virus.

In *Shares* stolid Deputy Secretary of State Robert Share has more diplomatic problems with his daughter and son than he does with foreign ambassadors and heads of state. Daughter Obie writes him vitriolic letters denouncing him for America's policy in Central America. Son Reg, like Jack in *A Father's Words*, is in his mid-thirties with nothing to show for it. He is filled with "filial turbulence" (164) and says with a smile that he came to his father's State Department office "to do [him] in" (164). Robert quickly responds that he does not think "that's in the realm of permissible things to say" (165). After this exchange, Reg leaves a note requesting that his father give him "$5,000. No questions" (167). Presumably Reg gets the money, for he next appears in Venice where his Uncle George is staying with his Share Companion, Bug Venerdy.

In Venice Reg seems to shed some of his Oedipal baggage. He says to Bug, "So I've had a gigantic figure in my life, and it's taken me years of shrinkwork to let me see that the giant's not only an ordinary man, but that it's I, on his shoulders, who made him gigantic. . . . It's awful what happens. Love becomes resentment, admiration envy" (170). But Reg is not completely cured of his aggressiveness. He cannot resist betraying his Uncle George by seducing Bug. Reg is less attracted to Bug at the end of the novel when the two are living together on Moorea, far from any father figure. Watching Reg watch the nude bathers (mostly German tourists), Bug realizes that "her body had no surprises for him, a far cry from Torcello" (180). Reg is equally destructive toward his father. With the success of the balloon rides, he becomes famous. When interviewed, Reg acts like "a prince of antidiplomacy, indiscreet, fluent and as full of quotable lines as a fig of meat" (174) – lines George realizes will hurt Robert's position in the State Department. Finally, when a bomb explodes on board one of his balloons, killing four people and of course downing Reg's business dreams, Robert Share also suffers in subtle ways in the corridors of power. Then Robert's wife, Eileen, gets pneumonia, "the first of the illnesses that marked her decline," and Robert leaves the State Department to become assistant general counsel to the Chemical Bank (180). Robert's Laius-like fears turn out to have been justified.

Death of Parents

Closely related to the theme of fatherhood in Stern's fiction is the experience many of the male protagonists have of losing their parents. In *Golk* Stern uses Poppa Hondorp's death to show how desensitized Hondorp has become: "Poppa Hondorp was burned to his ashes before sundown. Hondorp pled religious reasons for the rapidity although no prayers were said at the ceremony. Indeed, there was no ceremony. And no one – including Hondorp – was present but the men who carried in the body and carried out the ashes" (203). Hondorp fails also to send the *Times* a proper notice (the one he sends misspells his father's name and states that he has no survivors), "so Poppa Hondorp became one of the very few New Yorkers whose passing received no space at all in the great newspaper" (203). Hondorp does not even mention the death to Hendricks. When she finds out, she is horrified by his lack of feeling – "You're dead," she whispers in his face. "You're extinct" (204) – and decides to leave him. In *Natural Shocks* protagonist Fred Wursup's father commits suicide with his common-law wife (Wursup's real mother has for years been locked away in a mental institution).

When his mother and father died within six months of each other in 1978 and 1979, Stern turned the experiences into fiction, first in the stories "Dr. Cahn's Visit" and "Packages" and later in *A Father's Words*. In "Dr. Cahn's Visit" a son takes his senile physician father to the hospital to visit his wife who is dying of cancer. The father, whose speech is deformed by the vocabulary of bridge, asks if it is a good hospital, and the son reminds him that he – the father – was on the staff there for 50 years. Beneath the comic pathos of the father's forgetfulness is a harsher truth: "The most gentlemanly of men, Dr. Cahn's tongue roughened with his memory. It was as if a lifetime of restraint were only the rind of a wicked impatience" (*NR*, 136). Meanwhile, the son watches the mother's metamorphosis:

> Day by day, manners that seemed as much a part of her as her eyes – fussiness, bossiness, nagging inquisitiveness – dropped away. She was down to what she was.
> Not since childhood had she held him so closely, kissed his cheek with such force. "This is mine. This is what lasts," said the force. (137)

The reunion of the husband and wife, however, is the main focus of this story – a reunuion that is extremely brief and all the more moving because of Dr. Cahn's senility.

"Packages" has the same configuration of characters: senile father, dying (actually dead at the start and end of the story) mother, and son, but here the emphasis is much more on the son's ambivalence toward his mother, who, he confesses, was not his type. The feelings the narrator has toward his mother are complicated first of all by the fact that he knows he will inherit a lot of money when she dies. But even more, his ambivalence is fueled by years of estrangement: "Only at the beginning of my life and the end of hers did I love my mother wholly. When her life was over – like a simple-minded book – I pitied its waste" (365). What lends such power to the story is the unflinching honesty with which the son takes stock of his mother's life. He acknowledges her "intelligence" and "energy" but then adds, "Yet what was her life but an advertisement for idleness. And how could such a woman have failed to be a nagger, a boss, the idle driver of others, an anal neurotic for whom cleanliness was not a simple, commonsensical virtue but a compulsion nourished by her deepest need?" (365-66). These criticisms give way to other acknowledgments, however; that she was "the reliable, amiable center of a large group of women like herself, the one who remembered occasions and relationships, who knew *the right thing to do*" (366). These thoughts lead into an account of the heroic way in which she died, enduring the pain of cancer without protest: "She died bravely, modestly, with decorum. The decorum of practicality. (Her other tutelary deity.) She made up her mind to be as little trouble to those she loved as possible. (Cleanliness reborn as virtue.) She set her face to the wall, stopped taking medicine (without offending the nurses she loved so in the last weeks), and sank quietly into nonexistence" (366). In a shocking gesture, the son leaves the urn that contains her ashes in the garbage beneath "a plastic sack of rinds and fishbones" (360). Perhaps as a way of rationalizing the sacrilege, he says this is what she, "a child of the city," would have wanted – to have her ashes spead through the streets of Manhattan rather than lie in a Westchester mausoleum. Besides, he thinks to himself, "it was the *practical* thing to do," then asks, "*Wasn't it, Mother?*" (367).

Just as Stern gives a second, complementary version of his divorce in *A Father's Words*, so too does that novel depict once again the deaths of his parents. Cy's conflicted attitude toward his mother resembles that of the sons in "Packages" and "Dr. Cahn's Visit." Cy calls her "not just superficial . . . superfluous," despite her tendency to put on "terrific airs" (69). Still, he says, "there were spunk and hunger for life in her" (69). Cy's father is senile, devoted to the *Times*, which for him is always fresh because immediately forgotten, his "blue-green eyes, bright and indifferent as a roadside flower" (75-76). After his mother falls, breaks her hip, fails to heal, then gets diagnosed with cancer, Cy asks, "What is a mother?" He realizes that "for decades, we'd disagreed about almost every subject, every value, but those curls, those scallops, that fragrance, were

in some safe place, deeper, safer, more truly *me* than any disagree-
ment, any value" (80). Despite his mother's many faults, Riemer at
last finds sympathy for her narrow, orderly life – he even recognizes
that all she really wanted was "to live decently, to be respected, to
have some fun" (83).

For Stern, part of negotiating the death of his parents is facing
squarely the inevitability of his own death. As Stern has aged, so have
many of his protagonists, and Stern's real-life medical problems have
often been translated into the death scares of more than one Stern
hero. Wursup fears he may have cancer, as does Cy Riemer, who also
suffers from a paresophageal hernia in *A Father's Words*. In 1991
Stern underwent surgery to fix a paresophageal hernia of his own.
Before the operation his mind was dark with thoughts of mortality
(e.g., see his comments about dying in the 1988 interview in the
Appendix). After the successful operation Stern has regained his
enjoyment of life, as well as a desire to live a lot longer. Something of
this happier spirit is captured in "The Illegibility of the World." Narrator Larry Biel writes, "After my operation, I was so fatigued I didn't
care about living or dying. . . . Now I understand what I'd laughed at
in the obit column last week, the eighty-nine-year-old mogul,
William Paley, asking people why he had to die. I know life usually
wears you down and you're ready to go. Not with him. Not with me"
(*Shares*, 12).

If the death of his parents and his own health problems have
made Stern more aware of his own mortality, his grandchildren have
given him new hope for prolonged life, even life beyond the grave.
His orderly miscellany *The Position of the Body* is dedicated to Liza
Cady Baron, "who has already taught her grandfather much about
transmission and transfiguration"; *Shares and Other Fictions* is
dedicated to grandson Alexander Baron. In the lives of his children
and grandchildren, and in the works he has written for and about
them, rest Stern's dreams of continuity.

Chapter Nine

Portraiture

Every portrait reduces, simplifies, diminishes. ("The Degradation of Tenderness," *Shares*, 28)

Throughout his writing career Richard Stern has been fascinated by the various ways life and art mirror and sustain each other, the ways life gets captured or transmuted or distorted into art, as well as the ways art is shaped by life. As a realist, Stern hopes his fictions reflect and partake of the world's complexity. At the same time, he feels that one purpose of art, especially of narrative art, is to order and clarify and explain, to "convert the data of event into a coherence which doesn't just transform actuality, but creates it" (*IR*, 207). This power of narrative (and other kinds of art) to give meaning to the chaos of experience – a process Stern calls the "storification" of the real (and making "sense out of sensation") – is one of the things that distinguishes us as a species (*IR*, 201, 208). "We're all story makers," Stern writes, "constant inventors of the realities we call *our life*" (*IR*, 208).

Versions of the Real

Sometimes stories deliberately deflect, obscure, or deny obvious truths about the world, and Stern has often been drawn to situations that reveal a sharp contrast between reality and art that conceals reality. In "Cooley's Version," Stern's second published story (*Kenyon Review*, Spring 1954), a Harvard instructor named Cooley is given the job of translating the novels of French author Delphine Trèves. The longer he works on her manuscripts, the more he comes to admire her skill and beauty as a writer; he is therefore shocked when he sees her photograph for the first time in a book display: "There in the window, framed with his own rendering of her lucidities, her giant image glared at the street. He almost shuddered in

disbelief. There seemed no possibility that the gross lips and pen-
dulous cheeks swelling under steamy eyes could make up the physical instrument of the brilliant spirit he had let out into the American
air" (*Teeth*, 122). When he later meets her, the impression of the
photograph is confirmed. She eats like a "griffon" and spills coffee
on her publisher's lap (124); nevertheless, Cooley sleeps with her,
perhaps in an effort to find a fleshly correlative for the exaltation
produced in him by her books.

Art does not always conceal, however; sometimes it reveals
truths otherwise kept hidden. In the Borges-like story "Gardiner's
Legacy" a widow resurrects her husband's posthumous literary reputation despite her discovery as she reads through his journals, old
letters, and first drafts that he secretly loathed her and carried on
affairs with 86 different women. After Elinor Gardiner's death the
narrator can only marvel at her editorial skill and emotional restraint:
"He married her 'to marry Lilith,' and he called the union 'the marriage of Heaven and Hell.' Yes, I suppose that one could trace her
public utterances and find that every noble sentiment had been triggered by reading some viciousness of his" (*NR*, 189).

Life can also copy art. In his essay "Hunos and Historians,
Epigones and Dreamers" Stern recalls hearing for the first time
(while he was lecturing in Africa) about the John Hinkley, Jr., assassination attempt on Ronald Reagan: "It turned out the act had been
triggered by a work of art. I had been thinking of Reagan playing a
role and pitied him for stepping in where real bullets were shot into
real flesh, but this imitation of a movie assassination (the movie itself
influenced by the actual assassins of the sixties) was both fascinating
and repellent" (*PB*, 18-19). In another essay Stern contemplates the
precarious balance between thought and action, ideology and life,
when he examines the books in the apartment of slain Chicago black
power leader Fred Hampton: "A book man like me who feared,
hated, and only partly understood the violence of hunters and of
hunted felt it meant that the blood which lumped the mattress and
stained the floorboards was in part the blood of the books as well as
their readers" (*FH*, 72).

The most obvious examples of Stern's interest in the relationship
between life and art are his portraits of writers and other great
inventors. His first "orderly miscellany," *The Books in Fred Hampton's Apartment* (1973), includes short pieces on E. M. Forster,

architect Mies van der Rohe, and Flannery O'Connor, all written right after each died (each portrait appeared first in journals). At that time Stern felt he should avoid publishing his impressions of famous friends who were still alive:

> Since portraits are in a sense epitaphs . . . and one wants one's friends around alive, even kicking, one holds back. Anyway, alive they can digest your version and turn it into something ridiculously inadequate. (The modern saints – Gandhi, Dolci, and the like – seemed to enjoy shaking up the plaster versions of themselves. The most pathetic people are centerless bags of energy who constantly require commentators in order to know where they are.) Another reason for my restraint is fear of retaliation. A man as full of defects as this writer will be cautious. (*FH*, 202-3)

Such reticence is gone by the time of his second miscellany, *The Invention of the Real* (1982), which includes pieces on then living writers like Saul Bellow, Norman Mailer, C. L. Sulzberger, and Samuel Beckett, as well as the deceased Ezra Pound. *The Position of the Body* (1985) contains portraits of Philip Roth, Robert Lowell, and Lillian Hellman, the last two by then deceased. Stern's fourth orderly miscellany, *One Person and Another*, will offer a second piece on Beckett and one on Jacques Derrida; in addition, the collection will include a two-part essay on the forty-eighth annual International PEN Congress in 1986 (the essay appears in two separate issues of *Critical Inquiry* in Autumn 1986 and Summer 1988),[1] which is itself a compendium of lively thumbnail sketches. The brief, unflattering physical description of Joyce Carol Oates in the second of these essays ("Some Members of the Congress") brought from the subject an angry denunciation of Stern's "pig-souled sexism." Oates called the piece a "grotesquely homosocial piece of writing," "a hodge-podge of impressions."[2] This unexpected response (at least by Stern) no doubt confirmed his fear that sometimes a living subject will retaliate with a portrait of her own.

Not everyone agrees with Oates's appraisal of Stern's skill at drawing others. Writing about Stern's 1993 collection of essays, *One Person and Another*, Hugh Kenner praises the "uncanny" accuracy of Stern's literary portraits, "his gift for getting people to talk, especially reclusive people!" Kenner continues,

In his presentations, though he's self-effacing, still he's enough there to bring *you* there. Contrast Drummond's conversations with Ben Jonson, where we've ample record of Jonson's words but little sense of his presence, mainly because Drummond seems not present either. Or Spence's memoranda of Pope; same problem. But Stern brings the aged Pound to life; or the ailing Flannery O'Connor (even when she's absent, but writing inimitable letters). And those times with Saul Bellow! The very man speaks, while we hover, invisible. It nearly amounts to the invention of a new genre. Reporters interview such people, but haven't the sense to know what to record. Stern is enough of a novelist to know when not to invent.[3]

Stern's essay on Derrida, first printed in the *London Review of Books* (15 August 1991), is one of his masterpieces. More skeptical about his subject than in most of his portraits, Stern is still sympathetic enough to appreciate Derrida's sensitivity to language and to enjoy his charm as a person. At once critical and generous, distanced and engaged, the essay displays an easy familiarity with Derrida's difficult works and a subtle reading of unintentionally revealed signs about the man. The result is a nimble deconstruction of the father of deconstruction.[4]

The variety of portraits in Stern's stories and novels is impressive, ranging from *New York Times* obituaries to sculpted heads; from caricatures to published charges of treason; from the journals of angry wives to a psychiatrist's case studies of his children; from novels, films, and television shows based on the lives of real people to the images of others we all harbor in our heads. Stern appreciates the artistry of good portraiture, regardless of the medium, and several of his most memorable characters are skilled in the craft; at the same time his stories and novels are often about the dangers – and sometimes even the ethics and legality – of depicting real people. The dangers are not just those of hurting people's feelings and of subjects retaliating – though these are great restraints for most writers – but also the danger that the portrait will not be accurate, or will be accurate in some respects and therefore all-the-more misleading in others. Even worse is the danger that for the subject the portrait will be a kind of death, that artist and audience will prefer the clarifying simplifications of portraiture to the complexities of a real person. In Stern's fiction the theme of portraiture is enriched because many of the characters over the last 25 years are versions of himself and the people closest to him. He knows the benefits and drawbacks of mingling life and art as well as anyone writing fiction today.

Capturing Others

Stern's first great practitioner in the art of portraiture is Golk, who is motivated by satiric impulse, a desire both playful and malicious that is contaminated finally by his desire to reform society. His chosen medium, the hidden television camera, is perfectly suited to capturing his subjects unaware. But there is more to Golk's skill than a hidden camera; he creates situations that bring out his victims' flaws. His early skits, before "You're on Camera" goes national, depend on the element of surprise to catch his subjects off guard – for example, "people opening letters informing them that they'd been fired, children at the beach seeing their pails and shovels in the grip of sea monsters, women noticing suicidal types balanced on their living-room ledges" (*Golk*, 95).

A later, more advanced stage of "golkism" revolves "around scenes which somersaulted victims 'inside out and back again, from laughs to weeps to laughs'" (96). Right after Hondorp joins the crew, Golk's skits involve one of two strategies that depend on "thwarted appetite" (62). In the first, a prize is dangled in front of the victim, but when he or she attempts to grasp the prize, it turns to ashes (for example, the "Shakespeare golk" in the bookstore). The second strategy involves "stepping in between a man and his legitimate pleasures" (61). The goal behind these golks is the "arousal of . . . pure looks" and emotions that bring the victims' true natures to the surface in a "flash" (95). The final stage of golks, the exposing of corrupt public officials, goes well beyond such snapshots of people caught in states of pure feeling. The goal changes from a desire to portray to a desire to punish and transform.

Another genius of portraiture is the Pound-like sculptor Thaddeus Stitch. *Stitch*, in fact, is Stern's portrait of Pound as Stern saw him in the early 1960s. Stitch is old, losing his memory; he has not worked on his island of sculpture for two years. But he is able to accomplish a much smaller task when, against his own expectations, he completes a bust of Nina Callahan's head, which he dubs "Tenacity as Woman" (178). His harsh criticism of Nina's poem, while it may have been honest, reveals her true self, and this revelation inspires him: "In two good days he'd spotted what counted in her face. When he'd told her where the hollow was in her poem, he'd seen what counted rise up, and he'd gone home to put it into clay. Stony force. Yes, her sources were stone, she was not touchable, for all her concessions to gentleness. Her harmony, her peace were stone. It might suffice. Less had done beautifully. Sansovino was stony. And Jane Austen" (178). One irony of this passage is that Nina Callahan is modeled on Stern's friend Joan FitzGerald, who is herself a sculptor. Her bronze bust of Pound's head dominates Stern's Hyde Park living room.

Not all of the portraiturists are television wizards or great artists. Samuel Curry of *The Chaleur Network* wants to clear his son from a published charge of treason. Curry is "simply and absolutely" sure that Bobbie "could not have betrayed anyone in this world" (29). He also wishes to clear his own name, because he fears that people will see the son's treason as the father's (11). When he succeeds in getting Father Trentemille to publish a retraction, Curry revises false portraits of his son and himself. Nevertheless, he knows his new portrait of Bobbie is still – and will always be – far from complete: "what can a man know about another's life, what especially can a father know about his son's feelings, his – what he was. For five years now, off and on, I'd been finding out facts which would counter the notion that Bobbie was weak and traitorous. And I found facts, but I do not know what Bobbie was, hero or idiot, or whether he did more harm than good" (233). Cyrus Riemer of *A Father's Words* is another Stern protagonist who discovers his own reflection in his eldest son's. In Jack's failures, Cy sees not only his own guilt but also the qualities in himself he would rather leave buried. "If I'm unfair to Jack," Riemer says, "it's because I'm both his model and his despair; he's the dye which shows up my inadequacy. Every fault I think I've overcome – or hidden – shows up in Jack; in spades. Deliberate caricature? Maybe. But what a waste of life, an existence based on exposing what your father's concealed" (21).

Like Golk and Stitch, Fred Wursup of *Natural Shocks* is a professional portrayer of others. But whereas Golk lacks sympathy for his victims and Stitch tends to turn his subjects into abstractions (e.g., his bust of Nina becomes "Tenacity as Woman"), Wursup seems almost too sensitive to the feelings of those he captures. Skilled at forcing out what his subjects held back in interviews, Wursup had been praised by other journalists for the way he "intruded meanly into other lives" (73). The narrator explains that "the act of interviewing simplified, even brutalized, him. He became his readers, became the machinery of the medium: the presses needed ink, the air needed sound waves. Readers needed the diversion of other people's troubles" (73).

A few years before the action of the novel, Wursup suffered a bout of bad conscience after doing a piece for *Life* on reclusive filmmaker Hamish Blick (modeled on Samuel Beckett before Stern had actually met Beckett).[5] In the article Wursup compared the unattractive Blick to a Grünewald Christ and a Giacometti head, and *Life* had run the piece with juxtaposed photos of all three. When Blick wrote to *Life* protesting that "every law-abiding human has the right to keep his features – however amusing or repellent they may be – to himself and those he visits" (80), Wursup wrote a letter of apology. But to Wursup's surprise, Blick responded that Wursup had merely done "what [he] had to do" (81). Such endorsements aside, Wursup is tired of his "old methods" of "making stories out of little surgical cuts of appearance and talk"; he longs instead for something deeper – "long views" (21).

At one point in the novel Wursup tries to help his friend Jim Doyle out of a political jam. *Chouinard's News Letter* is about to print a story about Doyle's supposed neglect of his derelict father. Wursup gets wind of the damaging piece before it is published and decides to write a Doyle portrait of his own to counteract the negative one; he realizes the bad press could kill Doyle's run for his party's Senate nomination. Doyle had been one of the stars of Wursup's best-seller, *Down the American Drain*; the politician has mixed feelings about the book: he "had resented as well as taken advantage of the portrait Wursup had drawn of him in *Drain*. Favorable as it was, he'd felt himself confined by it, as if he had to maintain the portrait and was nothing more than what Wursup had noticed and written about" (130). After he publishes his second Doyle piece, Wursup worries that he has written a "political blurb"; he is embarrassed "to gush like this" and realizes he has done his friend more harm than good and certainly has failed to save his chances for the nomination

(167). True enough, Doyle is not even invited by the party chiefs to make a presentation.

If Wursup worries that he has engaged in paid hack work for a friend, he is even more concerned that he has become a parasite with Cicia Buell. He first meets her in a cancer ward while researching his article on death; a nurse had invited him, told him that "talking with a famous writer would cheer" the terminal patients (53). The more he gets to know Cicia, the harder it becomes for him to write the article. Perhaps he wants to avoid as long as possible the act of cannibalizing her death. In a painful scene the dying Cicia pulls off her wig, revealing a bare skull "studded with purple marks." When he tries to kiss her she says, "That's over for me" (235). So he comes downstairs, surrenders Cicia to death: "He'd toss off the article for Mike Schilp now. It was just another verbal turn. A hunk of subject he could chip into a lively piece. Another 'How To' piece" (237).

Perhaps the most fascinating portraiturist of all is Dr. Charlie Grasmuck, the psychoanalyst in "The Degradation of Tenderness," who publishes case studies of his son and his daughter in a professional journal. Charlie fails to anticipate the fury this exposure unleashes in his children. "It's the risk I took," he tells his friend and fellow analyst Anna, who narrates the story. "I must have known I was taking it" (*Shares*, 25). After receiving an angry letter from Alfred signed "Your repellent clown of a son," Charlie writes back:

> I printed what you call "portraits" and I call "case studies" not in the *Reader's Digest* or in *The New York Times*, but in a technical journal with a circulation of a thousand and a readership – judging from my own habits – half that.
>
> Your indictment, your anger, focuses on the fact that I used you and your sister as the subject of these case histories. Who else could I use? The whole point was that this was a father as well as an analyst examining, as honestly as he could, the parental relationship. Freud analyzed his children's dreams and experiences, and much of the civilized world is in his debt for it. If I am egregiously comparing myself to Freud, I respond, "What better model?"
>
> Have I violated "the confidentiality" of the parent-child relationship? I have. And I haven't escaped the pain of it. Your letter sees to that. (32)

The parallels with Stern the autobiographical writer are intriguing. Like Charlie, Stern has published warts-and-all "portraits" of his wives and children in the name of "artistic truth" – published them, again like Charlie, for relatively small audiences. As Charlie finds his model in Freud, Stern has looked to great writers like Proust and Joyce; neither of them ever let the feelings of family members compromise his art. And, finally, Stern has paid a terrible price within his family, especially after *A Father's Words*, for his own examination of "the parental relationship." Stern has not paid Charlie's price, of course. The responses of Charlie's children blew Charlie "out of the water" (24). It is no accident either that Charlie's son Alfred destroys his father's psychiatric practice, and eventually his father, by destroying his father's public image. "Charlie had been made ludicrous," explains the narrator. "Nothing worse for a psychotherapist" (36).

Caught in the Web

Stern is as fascinated by those who are captured as by those who capture others. When Hondorp sees himself on film for the first time in *Golk*, he "curl[s] like an ash. His voice, passing now directly to his ears instead of being modified by his cranial bones, was that of a vituperative whiner, a wavery sac of acid. It wrenched a groaning shudder from him" (35). When Golk later surprises Hondorp with footage of Poppa Hondorp, the son feels "his insides detach themselves from moorings and churn around until he [has] to grab a fold of his stomach to down the nausea" (74). For a while Hondorp manages to hide his discomfort from Golk – until, that is, Hondorp learns that Golk plans to air the scene: " 'You mean these little family scenes are shown to – to the public?' asked Hondorp, anger and amazement breaking down his controls" (77).

Being portrayed is not an unpleasant experience for everyone, however. Poppa Hondorp, like many of the older fathers in Stern's fiction, measures the success of a person's life by the size of his or her obituary in the *New York Times*. He is thrilled that Golk has captured him on camera, no matter that the poor doctor has been made to look like a sentimental fool. Hondorp cannot believe that "his father should relish the opportunity of being the butt of millions believing all the while he was the star guest of some forum programme. . . . It was incomprehensible to him" (79). But in language that anticipates Andy Warhol, Poppa Hondorp says to his son, "Want

it? Of course I want it. A private citizen, suddenly, by the caprice of
the gods, enjoying a vast forum like a man of public repute" (78-79).
In a similar way, Cicia Buell in *Natural Shocks* is pleased to have
Wursup do a story about her dying. When her friend Tina (a poet
who also "cannibalizes" Cicia's death [142]) complains about his
visits, Cicia says, "It's the closest I come to making poems. . . . I
describe what I didn't even know I thought. Otherwise, it's just drift,
and, you know, being scared, or drugged" (142). Wursup gets something from Cicia too; she teaches him about the limitations of any
specific portrait of herself, or for that matter, of anyone: "Can anybody stand just one version of himself? I mean, who wants to be just
described as Patient B? Or rich Miss Creep?" (145).

On the other side of these willing subjects, of course, stand
those who hate being captured, either because the portrait is false
and unfairly misleading or is accurate but unfairly intrusive. Hamish
Blick's shyness in *Natural Shocks* verges on the pathological. In the
midst of his interview he leaves Wursup and hides in his locked
house, refusing to emerge. A few years after the interview Blick
commits suicide, not because of Wursup's portrait but Wursup
knows his intrusion did not help the reclusive genius. After the story
on Jim Doyle appears, Doyle feels trapped, "spread out naked in the
millions or so most influential homes of America" (176). He fears
that Wursup has made him look like "a tragic clown" (177), but later
he writes to Wursup, "I'm not sure the piece did what we hoped it
would, but who knows if it's not better that way. I feel as if I'd been
seen by a fine painter. The piece has a kind of beauty independent of
me, and though I may not think I look quite like that, I respect it for
design, for feeling. I feel as if some of me was used in a work of fine
art" (181). Charlie's son Alfred in "The Degradation of Tenderness"
is less gracious after he reads the case study of himself his father
writes:

> Brilliance of insight? Yes, but not into what you're sighting.
>   Brilliance of style? I guess so. So what?
>   Down here, where it counts, in me, bad as I am, dumb as I am, nothing. No
> light, no help, no justice, and – of course – no mercy. (*Shares*, 31)

Readers might well wonder how close fictional Alfred's letter is to
ones Stern has received from his real children.

There are many other Stern characters who get unwittingly captured in unflattering poses or situations. Jeffrey Wendt of *Veni, Vidi . . . Wendt* and Robert Merriwether of *Other Men's Daughters* have their moral shortcomings and physical deformities recorded faithfully in the diaries of their disgruntled wives. Merriwether's affair with Cynthia Ryder is discovered to Merriwether's family when *Newsweek* reports a series of fires started by an American scientist named Brightsman who is working with Merriwether at the University of Nice. The *Newsweek* reporter just happens to mention "the Harvard Physiologist, Robert Merriwether" and "his pretty, young assistant, Cynthia Ryder" (*OMD*, 110).

The most interesting form of entrapment occurs when those who routinely capture others find themselves unexpectedly entrapped in the portraits of others. Poet Nina Callahan in *Stitch* keeps herself from starving in Venice by doing charcoal sketches in the Piazza. She admires the justice of her unflattering portrait of Edward Gunther, for which she charges him 10,000 lire (Cressida thinks it makes him resemble a "Nigerian sow" [174]). At first Nina is flattered by Stitch's desire to do her head, but then she sees what the old master sees in her: "He had made her into a kind of come-hither Celt. She did not pretend to beauty, but her face must show something more than he'd found there. He had made her look mechanical, abstract, device-like" (180).

Fred Wursup of *Natural Shocks* is another portrayer portrayed. After the success of *Down the American Drain* he finds that he is a minor celebrity who on television has "lost successive engagements as sit-down comic to talk-show hosts, actors, politicians, professors and poets" (21). He discovers also that he is fair game for hacks like the *New York Times*'s Ollie Fenchal, whose regular beat is the obituary page. Wursup "hit[s] the ceiling" when he reads Fenchal's account of him as "balding" and "brown-eyed," "a genial mollusc" whose "real existence is at his Smith-Corona" (49-50). His eyes, Wursup complains to the *Times* editor, are black, and he is not bald; furthermore, he uses a Remington Correcto, not a Smith Corona. "You know the game, Fred," the editor replies. "It always looks different on the other side of the pencil" (50). Fenchal's portrait of Wursup and the anger it provokes in its subject are an incredible anticipation of the unpleasant business with Joyce Carol Oates in *Critical Inquiry*.[6] Oates was so distressed by Stern's description of

her that she sent the journal a photograph to prove that she is neither thick-lipped nor "neurasthenic" (Oates, 194).

Perhaps the most ironic victim of portraiture in the Stern canon
is Cyrus Riemer of *A Father's Words*, who sees himself turned into
the philandering, "Addled Intellectual" father on son Jack's television show (183). Riemer is not exactly a portraiturist himself, though
he is clearly one of Stern's versions of himself (hence the irony of his
being victimized in this way). In another sense, however, we are all
portraiturists, even though not all of us publish or hang in public our
images of others. Our real lives go on in other people's heads, Stern
has said, citing a passage in Conrad's preface to *A Personal Record*
(see Appendix). At one point Jack says to his sister Jenny, "He knows
me through my faults. It's as if he's sealed off that part of me and
preserves it. He only had three digits of my number" (*FW*, 41-42).
After Riemer sees Jack's show, he compares his son's portrait of him
to what F. Scott Fitzgerald imagined might be "the shoe's version of
van Gogh" (187). Jack responds that Riemer has not painted his
(Jack's) portrait, to which Riemer says, "I think you think I have. I've
had this version of you, have thought about you in a certain way,
have spoken to others about you that way, maybe even persuaded
you that that's the way you are. I think you've resented it, and that
this is your way of getting back at me" (188).

Although Jack is not sure he buys his father's theory (he had not
even realized he based the father on the show on Cy), Riemer offers
to forgive him, perhaps as author Stern hopes to be forgiven by
those whom he has portrayed: "what the hell, where else should you
draw characters from but people you know, people you feel strongly
about? I just wish you didn't feel about me the way it shows up"
(188). At least Riemer has the inner strength to draw his own portrait, to resist having his identity imposed on him by others. That
same strength of self-definition is one Stern hopes for and admires in
members of his family and in friends who have at times felt injured
by his art.

Chapter Ten

A Place on the Map

"To make the complex clear is a beautiful as well as a useful thing. To represent depth on a surface. Beautiful." (*A Father's Words*, 77)

Richard Stern has enjoyed a career that would be the envy of most people who try to write fiction. He has won prestigious prizes and has been praised by many important writers and critics. Yet even his most ardent supporters acknowledge that Stern has not reached as large an audience as they – and he – would like. They also concede that he has more often been excluded from than included on the critical establishment's list of major American fiction writers since World War II. As long ago as 1970 Philip Roth wrote that "of America's most under-appreciated novelists, probably none is neglected with such thoroughgoing regularity, with such dedication, as Richard Stern. It's appalling. . . . Maybe the reviewers are diligently off reading all the wonderful new novels about the student revolution. For a vacation some time they might try Stern on the revolutions of the cerebral burgher, on which he's simply brilliant."[1]

Sadly, little has changed since Roth's blistering statement. Peter S. Prescott wrote in *Newsweek* in 1986 that Stern is "one of this country's best-kept secrets" (Prescott). In his 1989 review of *Noble Rot* Sven Birkerts observes that Stern is "hardly a household name," then asks, "In an era when writers barely old enough to drive are garnering enormous advances and, worse, enormous reputations, how is it that a writer of Stern's caliber still waits for recognition?" (Birkerts, 46). Though Stern himself is understandably tired of hearing about his lack of fame, he has contributed to his reputation as a writer who is famous for not being famous. He once even called himself "a has-been without ever having been a been" (Spencer, 4).

To promote Stern's greater popular acceptance and greater recognition from scholars and canon-setters as I have done in this study is not to ignore the difficulties, chief of which is that his work

139

can be difficult. Though he is a lot more accessible than many people imagine, Stern is not for all markets, not for hard-core action-thriller or mystery fans or for readers of supermarket romances (Stern once half-seriously wished his books were sold in the A & P [Birtwistle, 184]), or for the politically correct of either the left or the right. Rather than the simple oppositions many of these popular genres and ideological stances afford, Stern's works are usually animated by irony, complexity, and paradox. His fiction can be difficult because so often it is based on a strategy of "contra-diction," of voices opposing other voices. Not all of Stern's contradictions, of course, are the result of a deliberate artistic strategy. Some are unintentional, bound up with the personality of the author.

Stern's attitude toward fame is itself curiously ambivalent. He has made celebrity a motif in several novels and is known to seek out famous people when he travels. His literary portraits, of course, offer ample evidence of this interest. He has also had the chance to observe the celebrity of his close friends Philip Roth and Saul Bellow. Though Stern has had moments of wishing their kind of popularity for his own works, he has always been unwilling to take all the steps necessary to achieve bestsellerdom. He has claimed that he would not know how to write a best-seller, so he does not try. He writes for himself and hopes, or even assumes, the best of his readers.

Is Stern elitist, or, on the contrary, does he think too highly of average readers, their intelligence and range of reference? His novels and stories are filled with intelligent nonacademics: Peter Biel, a vinyl-cone salesman who reads Kafka in "The Illegibility of the World" (or his retired salesman father, Larry); Arthur Powdermaker, the photographer's model in "Zhoof" who travels frequently to Europe to see "Cézannes, Monets, Manets, Bonnards, Pissarros" (NR, 304), as well as the birthplaces of Dürer and Wagner; Tommy Buell, a glass manufacturer and would-be author in *Natural Shocks*; and George Share in *Shares*, a college drop-out who is known in his community as the "Shoe Store Plato" (*Shares*, 114). Such characters reflect Stern's belief in the intellectual curiosity and ability of people outside the university, and this belief no doubt encourages him not to condescend.

Stern's love of autodidacts notwithstanding, he knows most average readers prefer not to stretch themselves. For one thing, he has his disappointing sales figures for most of his books, as well as the consequent frequent changes of publishers. On occasion he has even offered parodies of his high-minded approach to his art. In the story "East, West . . . Midwest," for example, historian-translator-journalist Bidwell writes an article on students for *Midland*, a Sunday newspaper supplement. The article attempts to get across "an idea of the complexity of the matter" by listing issues raised by students around the world, "the lighting system at Prague Tech., the language question at Louvain and Calcutta, football at Grambling, political issues at Hamburg and Berkeley"; added to this is "a tail of explanations from commentators, Aron, Howe, Feuer, McLuhan, and a handful of college presidents" (*NR*, 98). His editor, Shiffrin, is not pleased; to him the piece is "Bidwell's usual academic glop which turned every second piece he touched 'into the *Britannica*'" (98).

In a passage that has obvious relevance to Stern, Bidwell reflects, "Of course, he [Shiffrin] was right, was always right. To most of their readers, Joey Bishop was Einstein, the amount of information that could be ladled out in any one story should not exceed a recipe for French toast" (98). Thus Shiffrin advises him, "Look, find some little spade chick on the Circle campus, let her yack away half a column, then get some yid prof to yack up the other half, a few pictures, and we got our story. Save this truckload of cobwebs for the *Atlantic Monthly*" (*NR*, 98). Perhaps even closer in attitude to Stern than Bidwell is Kevin Miyako, editor of *Chouinard's News Letter* in *Natural Shocks*: for Miyako, "ignorance permitted the handsomest assessment of their readers" (41).

Another seeming contradiction in Stern is his attitude toward women – at least some women have observed a problem. Joyce Carol Oates, for example, accuses Stern of sexism in his second essay on the 1986 PEN conference, "Some Members of the Congress," especially when Stern reports that he complained to Arthur Miller about those "fucking bitches" – feminists whose protests disrupted the proceedings (871). And there are male characters in Stern who indulge in what one reviewer called "misogynist metaphysics" (*Kirkus*). Furthermore, Stern committed the ultimate sexist sin (at least in the eyes of some feminists) by leaving his middle-aged wife and four children for a student half his age. He even had the nerve to write a book about his marital treason.[2]

Stern states in "Some Members of the Congress" that he has an "internal confidence" that he does not have "an ounce of chauvinist blood" in him, "at least in [his] intellect," though he does concede that he is "a creature of an obsolete tradition" (871-72). He points out also that he was "the earliest reader" he knows of *The Second Sex* and that many of his female characters are "creatures of liberated intelligence; theirs and mine" (872). He is on record as a champion of contemporary poetry written by women, which he thinks is the most exciting thing on the literary scene today.[3] Stern would hardly deny that some men in his fictions express sexist thoughts and emotions; such thoughts and emotions are natural consequences, he would say, of living in these confusing, sexually unsettling times. As for his marital treason and the book that resulted from it, Stern likes to refer to Susan Braudy's review in *Ms.* that praises the novel for its fairness to its three main characters, not just protagonist Robert Merriwether, but also wronged wife Sarah and new lover Cynthia. "Happily for literature and for women's politics," Braudy writes, "this tale is not another novel like Norman Mailer's *American Dream*, in which male orgasm is personified and developed into the book's most sympathetic character. Richard Stern's *Other Men's Daughters* is an emotionally and intellectually profound novel with three vital, wonderfully drawn characters" (39).[4]

Another problematic aspect of Stern's art is its autobiographical nature. Many authors write about their lives. What makes Stern's practice controversial is its currency. He is not writing about his early childhood but about his feelings and relationships from last week, yesterday, and today. A number of questions arise: Where does Stern the artist connect with Stern the person with relationships? Which self is more important to him? How does each self affect the other? If his art is enriched in thought, feeling, and verisimilitude because he writes about his own life, how is that life affected by being the subject of his fiction? Are his relationships improved as a result? Or is fiction-writing an implement of oppression within the family, a way to control those closest to him with the threat of exposure? Do the real-life family bruises raised by his fictions become the subject of new autobiographical fictions? He has already made the evils of autobiographical fiction a theme in his autobiographical fictions.

Should Stern be praised for his unsparing honesty and artistic courage, as Joyce and Proust have been praised? Or should he be condemned for callousness? Probably no one could be as hard on him as he has been on himself. In his essay "The Debris of a Novel" Stern acknowledges that "the heart" of *A Father's Words* "was – is – a transfiguration and projection of the author's relationships to two wives and four children" (*PB*, 180). After this confession he makes an extraordinary promise not to write about family matters again: "I think I'm finished now with family novels. I've hurt everyone I can hurt. Not – as far as I know – trying to hurt, but there it is, and I paid for it with the thousands of pages, the thousands of hours wasted, the typed excursions to Africa and Tulsa, the hearts and pockets of inventions I'll never use. I was punished for failing to see my subject. I must get another" (*PB*, 180). Despite this pledge *Shares and Other Fictions* continues a number of autobiographical motifs, especially the Oedipal rivalry between father and son.

Yet another complexity is Stern's attitude toward politics and art – inherited to some degree from New Criticism and from modernists like T. S. Eliot and James Joyce. Stated simply, that attitude frowns on art with any purpose beyond itself. Stern is one of the few writers on the contemporary scene who take the esthete's high road and speak openly of "fountains of artistic bliss" afforded by great works of art.[5] At the same time, he disparages the politicization of postmodern criticism, its tendency to read against the grain of an author's obvious intentions.

Stern is also unhappy about the recent Foucauldian trend toward "squeezing authors out of their texts" ("Penned In," 1); in one essay he even wonders nostalgically whether "the old hierarchy of great artist, professional interpreter, and student" is "intrinsically bad" ("Old Humanists"). Such reactions from creative writers against postmodern criticism are hardly unexpected. What is surprising is that Stern is – and has always been – so good at reading "against the grain" of other authors. After all, he was one of the first and only reviewers to pan Joseph Heller's *Catch-22*.[6] Perhaps that review is less a matter of reading against the grain than of invoking a higher literary standard. But his recent essay on Jacques Derrida in the *London Review of Books* does unto Jacques what deconstructionists have often done unto others.

Although Stern eschews art that is organized to promote a political agenda or ideology, there is often an undeniably political dimension to his art, a dimension more subtle and complex than the simple idea that political quiescence amounts to an endorsement of the status quo. Stern has long been fascinated with politicians and government officials. His essay "The Pursuit of Washington," for example, provides an amusing account of his difficulties meeting with John Kennedy and Richard Nixon in 1959. *Europe: Or Up and Down with Baggish and Schreiber* and *The Chaleur Network* both briefly explore the nightmare of Nazi Germany and the Holocaust, as in their different ways do stories like "The Good European" and "Zhoof." *Stitch* offers a portrait of Ezra Pound, whose art and life became contaminated by fascism. And in *Shares* Stern explores the mind of Deputy Secretary of State Robert Share, who receives a letter from his daughter Obie condemning America's actions in Nicaragua. As a private citizen, Stern has at times been political, especially during the Vietnam War when he was outspoken about his hatred of American policy and Lyndon Johnson. He spent time with Robert Kennedy on the 1968 campaign trail and speaks admiringly of the slain politician. He votes in local and national elections, reads newspapers and watches "MacNeil-Lehrer," signs petitions, even writes angry letters occasionally. He wrote an op-ed essay on Senator Alan Simpson's muddled misquoting of Shakespeare during the Clarence Thomas hearings. Two stories in *Shares and Other Fictions*, "The Illegibility of the World" and "The Anaximander Fragment," contain references to the recent war with Iraq ("Anaximander" is actually set in Saudi Arabia during the war).

In place of a political ideology Stern's work provides a vision of the world, as well as values that derive from that vision. The key is complexity. Many of Stern's heroes are people who try to make sense of life without ignoring, denying, or reducing its complexity. Some of his characters go further: they clarify things not only for themselves but for others. In *Natural Shocks* journalist Fred Wursup participates in the process of shrinking the world's million happenings to the daily bread of newspapers, yet he has a genuine commitment to accuracy, to getting "things right" (32). Cyrus Riemer of *A Father's Words* edits a scientific newsletter that makes complex ideas accessible to lay readers. (This skill does not prevent Cy from occasionally getting lost in confusions of his own devising. "You complicate things so, Dad," says his daughter Livy. "I wonder why. Maybe because you've spent so much time clarifying other people's work" [111].) Robert Share finds his "vocation" in keeping the world "reasonable and orderly" (*Shares*, 129); he finds "something beautiful about the way the world was reduced for him" by the assistants who write lucid page-length briefs on trouble spots around the globe (131). Of course, Stern knows the danger of such clarifications as well as their beauties. "Order for its own sake was ruinous," thinks Fred Wursup in *Natural Shocks*. "(At Auschwitz, the motto was *zauber machen* – 'clean up.') Madness tried to conceal itself with order" (68).

This business of clarifying, according to Stern, is one of the purposes of literature; paradoxically, another "of the social jobs of literature is complicating what we think about and experience" (*FH*, 202). For both purposes, Stern feels the need for the transmission of great art from one generation to the next. As chaotic and dangerous and depressing a time as our age has been, it would be a million times more chaotic, dangerous, and depressing without the sweetness and light of artistic endeavor. There can be no doubt that Stern sees himself as a link, however tenuous, in the great tradition; nor can one doubt his sincerity in fearing that the tradition is in danger of passing into oblivion.

In the face of the world's complexity, Stern's fiction promotes a generosity of spirit and human sympathy, a desire to understand rather than simply condemn or judge. "*Tout comprendre, tout pardonner*" is the motto for at least two of his protagonists – Samuel Curry of *The Chaleur Network* and Holeb of "Ins and Outs," as it probably is for Stern as well. Perhaps it is this awareness of complexity that leads Stern to value other qualities as well: tenacity and perseverance, tolerance, the ability to learn and grow, and, above all, the ability to love. Whether it is Merriwether's refusal to live a life without intimacy in *Other Men's Daughters* or Riemer's agonizing concern for his children in *A Father's Words*, the capacity to love, even more than the capacity to understand, is the final measure of any character in Stern.

Many writers express similar ideas and endorse similar values; many, like Stern, have their hearts in the right place. Stern, of course, has something else, the skills of a talented artist, the intuitive sense of form, the assurance of voice, and the seriousness of purpose to put his gifts to use. For those who love the beautifully turned phrase, the sculpted sentence or paragraph, the flashes of insight and wit, the charm and humanity of so many of his characters, there is really nothing quite like Richard Stern's fiction.

So, I say, give Richard Stern a place on the map. Which map? Give him a place on the big map – the map of major fiction writers in America in the second half of the twentieth century. He has devoted his life to literature, produced 16 books (and counting) of very high quality, including some of the finest short stories and novels of our age. He has shown remarkable consistency over time, remarkable honesty, remarkable integrity. He has waited patiently, modestly, to be read and reread. Put him on the big map. Such dedication and achievement deserve no less.

Appendix: An Interview with Richard Stern

The questions and answers that follow are drawn from interviews that took place at Stern's home in Hyde Park, Chicago, on 3 and 5 June 1988, two years after the publication of *Father's Words* and seven months before the release of his story collection *Noble Rot*. During both interview sessions Stern seemed – for him – unusually subdued, troubled. For one thing, he was still mourning the wasted time and pages he spent on *Father's Words*; he feared he was having similar problems (of finding the real subject) with his then-novel-in-progress, *Shares*. Stern was also upset by recent claims about the extent of Ezra Pound's anti-Semitism by Robert Casillo in *The Genealogy of Demons: Anti-Semitism, Fascism, and the Myths of Ezra Pound* (1988) and by Jerome McGann in a series of lectures on Pound delivered at the University of Chicago.[1] Stern's fourth novel, *Stitch*, was inspired by his acquaintance with Ezra Pound in Venice in 1962-63 (Pound is the model for Stitch, the book's brilliant octogenarian sculptor).

The interviews had their moments of comedy as well as gloom. During one session Stern's second wife, poet Alane Rollings, entered the study to announce that she had just approached someone in an information booth at the Hyde Park Art Fair, only to realize at the last possible moment that the someone was Stern's first wife, Gay Clark Stern. The two women have never met, despite having lived within a few blocks of one another for many years. After a few moments of amazed laughter (and shouts from Stern of "Oh my! Oh my!") about the close call at the information booth, Stern asked Rollings what she bought at the art fair. She dutifully produced an oversized, glazed mug.

"Some mug," said Stern appreciatively, looking not at the ceramic monstrosity but at Rollings instead.

James Schiffer: If you were writing a book about your fiction, what would you say?

Richard Stern: Oh boy, that's very difficult. It's wonderful to see what intelligent readers have to say about my work. But it's usually not what I see. Obviously, there are secret meanings for me that I can't divulge. I know things that I don't expose, and try not to expose.

Schiffer: The story of the story. But what about the meanings that are accessible to intelligent readers?

Stern: I'm affected by intelligent criticism; I'm able to read a book in this way and take pleasure in it, and when another reading comes along I take pleasure in that and see the book that way. An unfavorable reading comes along and I say "OK." But there are personal things behind certain pages. I can remember writing a certain page while I felt a certain way, translating something in myself and being relieved of pressure. But I don't know that that makes any critical sense.

Schiffer: Are you sensitive to reviews?

Stern: I certainly read them. And I remember a lot of them. As far as their controlling my work or my trying to alter my work because of them, no. In a way I've been lucky not to get so much attention. It's clear – to me – that [John] Updike has been responding to his critics. I have not been hurt all that much. The big thing has been not being read . . . that's a big hurt. You have to develop a callus for it, or you can't live.

Schiffer: You have a reputation as a difficult writer. Is your work difficult because you have too high a regard for the reading public? Do you overestimate the average reader's tastes and intelligence?

Stern: I've been told this by people. I think there's something else. Some of my work is not sufficiently articulated. There's not enough explanation. There's a little too much joy in obliquity. It is a joy, a genuine joy, but that's an exclusive kind of joy. I'm not sure I like it. And I don't know quite what to do about it. I think it's part of the reason I take so long with books. I have all this stuff, then come the years of trying to find the subject in it. I'm having trouble now – I'm at the point of burning the work of the last two years . . . three year's worth of work. Even though I left out lots of the stuff that I said was going to be in it.

Schiffer: I recall a review of *1968* by D. A. N. Jones that complained about the complexity of your prose. Do you remember? He called your style "Butch academic." [Stern laughs.] But I've been reading [Jacques] Derrida lately, and let me tell you, compared with his style, yours is a glass of water.

Stern: Derrida and Heidegger, whew. Did you read Derrida's piece on Paul de Man in *Critical Inquiry*?[2] That wonderful confession that he has never known how to tell a story, and then the story comes in despite that.

Schiffer: *Stitch* has that obliquity.

Stern: In *Stitch*, yes, I had Pound. I try to capture his oblique devices in *Stitch*. If he can do it, I thought, I can do it . . . and so . . . the son of a bitch seduced me. But I still care for his work. I still believe in it. The modernists are still my heroes. Which doesn't mean I can't read Hemingway's grandson [Raymond] Carver. I read one of his stories two days ago. It is a good story. There's an obliquity in it too. But it's . . . simpleminded. I mean, it deals with powerful emotions in simple people which cause them to make significant gestures. (Which are often misinterpreted.) And in the end there's some little grope or debacle or some gesture of futility. That's not enough for me. Perhaps that's why Carver's biography is so jammed up against his stories. It is a moving story. I like the man (whom I met but twice). Amy Hempel, Mary Robison. They also do wonderful, shorthand stories.

Schiffer: Do you see these people, these minimalists, descending from Hemingway?

Stern: Oh, Hemingway is so beautiful. He's so rich. He gets the sensuous content of things, and they seldom bother with it. The real stuff going today is poetry by women, Sharon Olds writing about sex, or her feelings for her father, or her daughter, having a baby and all that. That's big stuff. And Alane's wonderful poems.

Schiffer: Most of your stories and novels are from the male point of view, but you have done some stories and parts of novels from the point of view of women.

Stern: Yes. I want to be able to do women. In *Noble Rot* I was conscious about alternating the stories with the woman's point of view: "Teeth," "Wanderers," "The Ideal Address," "Recital for the Pope," and "Troubles." When *Other Men's Daughters* came out, there was a review in *Ms.* which said it was rare for a male writer to capture a woman's point of view so well.

Schiffer: That must have been gratifying.

Stern: It was very gratifying . . . because someone in Texas had dumped on the book as chauvinist. I try to be careful at this point in my life. Fiction does help iron out your passions.

Schiffer: When I look at the early part of your career, say from 1960 to 1965, when you published all those books in rapid succession – *Golk; Europe; Teeth, Dying and Other Matters; In Any Case;* and *Stitch* – what strikes me most is the incredible variety of these works. Were you consciously trying not to repeat yourself?

Stern: I can't think that I was consciously trying with each book to come up with something different. It's just that there are so many things in the world. For some reason something becomes a story. I don't know that there's much more than that. I don't think that there's much consciousness. I know that at various times things have happened to show me that X, Y, and Z are really all versions of A. I had a dream, an amazing dream about 20-odd years ago, in which I was in a field. Cauliflowers started throwing themselves at my head. It made me realize that I had been writing stories in which there where large-breasted, dominating women, and that they were all my mother. This was in the dream. Then I made a conscious effort not to have such women in my fiction.

Schiffer: At the core of your novels *Golk* and *Stitch* are the title characters who are in each case great inventors. Where does this theme come from? Also the technique that you use, of approaching the great man indirectly, obliquely, as you do in *Golk* and *Stitch*.

Stern: *Anna Karenina, The Sun Also Rises, Madame Bovary.*

Schiffer: What about the great inventors?

Stern: My whole life I've pursued these people. What is the best, the most interesting thing going? By chance I have run into them. By chance. I mean, whether I'm walking through the park and seeing Sinclair Lewis when I'm 12 years old. Or Einstein in Central Park. Or [Artur] Schnabel. What are they about? I knew that I never wanted to write about a writer. The closest I came, I suppose, is in *Natural Shocks* and *A Father's Words*. But these protagonists are not great inventors. So there's the problem of how to put one of those guys down. (With Stitch I have a great old guy. Debris.) I spent my life reading these people. So what are they like? But I had to approach them indirectly. Who's done it directly? I'm not sure any modern author does it. I don't think [Romain Rolland's] *Jean-Christophe* is a great book. [Thomas Mann's] *Doctor Faustus* is at least a good one, and Mann uses the narrator as a reflector.

Schiffer: You once told me that the period from 1965, when you published *Stitch*, to 1970, when you published *1968*, was the most difficult of your writing career. Was there any relation between your feeling stuck after *Stitch* and your turning to autobiographical material? Was it a response to critics?

Stern: Not in reaction to critics. It was a feeling of helplessness coupled with a sense of, "Look, this is what comes back again and again to you. Why reject it?" I couldn't do anything else.

Schiffer: When did you first decide to use the materials of your own life in your fiction? Are you in Gunther, the American in Europe in *Stitch*, or is *Veni, Vidi . . . Wendt* the turning point? There is clearly a lot of you in the composer Wendt.

Stern: Wendt certainly opened me up. I don't know why. The early works are mostly "out there." There's a version of myself in *Europe*, a minor character, Horstmann. I remember making him unpleasant.

Schiffer: Schreiber and Baggish in *Europe* are "out there"?

Stern: Schreiber and Baggish are out there. Hondorp in *Golk* . . . I mean, there are certain elements of myself, especially in his relation to his father. If anything, though, it's my father's relationship to his father. At a certain point things started to come inside. I just let it happen. Why do I write about four children? It's a number I work well with, a number I understand. There is the work which comes out of the family, the wife, the divorce, the Alane figure, the power and complexity of paternal feelings.

Schiffer: That's also a theme in one of your early novels, *In Any Case* [reissued as *The Chaleur Network* in 1981].

Stern: That's right. And there's something else in *In Any Case*. The treason. Tom Rogers once pointed out that that was in the earlier books too. Hondorp turning on Golk. Baggish and Tiberius betraying Schreiber. The fear of, the agony of, betrayal of those close to one. That's a powerful feeling.

Schiffer: And it's a repeated motif. In *Natural Shocks* protagonist Fred Wursup's best friend and editor, Will Eddy, has had an affair with Wursup's ex-wife, an affair that Wursup never learns about. There's a similar combination of partnership and sexual betrayal in the story "Double Charley." Where does this come from, this fear of betrayal?

Stern: I'm not sure I can talk about it. I'm obviously troubled by my own allegiance to Pound (himself an official traitor). As I was reading the Casillo book, I wanted to go down in the middle of the night and remove that bust of Pound from the living room. I said, "My God, is this what he was doing all that time?" Then I said, "But look, your impressions counted. He was not that way with you. And this is the work of Joan FitzGerald, your friend, and it's a beautiful thing." I mean, I'm just getting into this theme of treason from another angle. Also anti-Semitism, which should have been in front of my face all my life. Since it wasn't, does that mean I've betrayed something? What have I run away from? What's the evasiveness in this Jewish business? Well, "Zhoof" is one answer to that. "Zhoof" happened to me on a train. I faced it.

Schiffer: That moment where you Jewish protagonist Powdermaker wonders what gave him away, what "Jewiness" in himself made the couple leave the dining car on the train because Powdermaker was there? That's incredibly powerful.

Stern: A friend of mine said it's inconsistent that Powdermaker is a model. How can a model think like this? I said, "But that's it." He's made a living from the most superficial part of himself, exhibiting himself, and he now sees how much he's stayed on the surface of life despite the fact that he's tried to be serious by traveling and reading and so on. Now he's been brought up short. He's down where it really counts. The anti-Semite has been precious to him.

Schiffer: The theme, in a way, is Jewish anti-Semitism. Or at least the dilemma of feeling paranoia about the gentile world and shame about the Jewish one. How much of that goes into your relationship with Pound? How much of your attraction was because he was an interesting old man, and a famous one? How much because he was a known anti-Semite?

Stern: That's right. You beard the anti-Semite. You seek out the anti-Semite and say, "How can you? Here I am."

Schiffer: In *Stitch* the Pound character – Stitch – is very rude to Gunther, just as Pound had been rude on one occasion with you. And in the novel there's the suggestion that maybe the reason for the outburst is that Gunther's a Jew.

Stern: Yeah, there's a suggestion.

Schiffer: And maybe Pound's rudeness to you was his anti-Semitism.

Stern: Maybe.

Schiffer: And you're still not sure?

Stern: [Pause] No. I'm not sure.

Schiffer: And are you close to saying, "What's the difference?"

Stern: Well, I'm saying that people are so complicated. There's everything in them, in us. But I'm not gonna be stuck on it as I think [Saul] Bellow and [Philip] Roth sometimes are. Bellow has said to me, "You never recognize anti-Semitism." We got into an argument about the Gore Vidal piece in the *Nation*.[3] "Of course he is, Richard. You never see it." But I do see it. Yet there's an element of truth in what he says.

Schiffer: It's like the Derrida piece on [Paul] de Man's anti-Semitic essays. There's a parallel with your portrayal of Pound.

Stern: There is. It's fascinating. After all, this is a guy [de Man] who did this when he was 20.

Schiffer: But then you hear it about Pound, and he's not 20; he's 60.

Stern: I had studied Pound and taught his work. I used to read the terrible radio broadcasts to my students, but I didn't realize – until I read the Casillo book – how important anti-Semitism was to him.

Why should I be taking this up now? I who have spent a life saying "the hell with that moronic crap."

Schiffer: Well, is the question why you didn't see it earlier?

Stern: What is it in me? What is there in me? As I say, in "Zhoof" I faced it. What is there for me to do now? There's nothing for me to do. My characters are all Christians now. I don't know how I'll deal with it. I don't want to deal with it.

Schiffer: It touches on that whole issue of art and politics . . .

Stern: And betrayal.

Schiffer: Does it matter to Pound's work?

Stern: Jerry McGann came up here and gave three or four lectures. Called Pound a "poet of hate" and said that fascism was crucial to him. I said that first of all, fascism was many things. There were even good parts of it. I said Pound was not just a poet of hate. The point is that this started me off. Then I read the Derrida piece on de Man and two days later the Casillo book. I'm much interested now in obsession. I spoke with an analyst about it, how it is often a safety valve for other troubles. And I've been writing about hatred a little bit and what it is. There are different types. There's useful hatred and not useful. So all this stuff is whirling around and I'm trying to make sense of it.

Schiffer: Speaking of making sense, I like your understated preface to *Noble Rot*. Are you usually reluctant to comment on your work?

Stern: I've seen people who get asked much more frequently. Say, Bellow. He uses such as occasion for a kind of aria or soliloquy – a brilliant pitch. Which doesn't mean that what he says isn't correct. Even Hemingway went too far. I read the preface to the *49 Stories*, which is one of the great books as far as I'm concerned. He says this story was written here and this one was written there, and "I like this town and that town." Who cares? So what? All these prefaces. Prefaces move the reader from the stories. Prefaces are an insult – no, not an insult, a superfluity. We all love gossip, but it smudges the work. One great thing about being a fiction writer is that you make an object, and the object isn't you. It's more attractive and interesting than you, and you don't know what it is.

Schiffer: I wonder if that's why Shakespeare drew so often on already existing stories.

Stern: Boy, what a relief. Updike is doing that with his [Nathaniel] Hawthorne updates. I'm nervous about that sort of thing. I don't know if it's a form of laziness in me, but I think it has something to do with inner direction, the point where you *feel* the work. Take the book I'm writing now. I'm beginning to feel the play of the two brothers against each other, the public life of the assistant secretary of state, the private life of his brother. At this point I'm relying more on the rhythm of counterpoint. This morning I was looking at a Degas painting of a friend who was an oboist in an orchestra. I noticed that in this orchestra the sections are all mixed up. The modern orchestra keeps the instruments separate – the violins here, the cellos there. That's been a difficulty of mine. I had to learn in *A Father's Words* to group the instruments, concentrate the force, not mix up, scatter, or be elusive.

Schiffer: What is it in a writer that tells him – that tells you – this paragraph goes and that one stays?

Stern: The principle of inclusion. The organizing principle. With *A Father's Words* everyone saw what it was except me. Family stuff. I wanted to make a comprehensive novel. I finally had to throw all the excess bags out. I was trying to evade everything in myself that counted. The core was this story. The last 10 years I've been having more trouble finding the story. I've always had trouble, though *Golk* was written fairly quickly. *Europe* I only saw when a friend of mine, Mike Zwerin, taught me about numbers. Part 2. Part 3. What a lift that was.

Schiffer: What are your thoughts on the difference between writing stories and writing novels?

Stern: The first thing is knowing when you're not making sense, when you don't have the material for a novel. The novella in *1968*, *Veni, Vidi . . . Wendt*, and the long story ["Idylls of Dugan and Strunk"] were on their way to becoming novels. I thought there was enough material. You had several people. They had interesting careers and they were connected and so on. I forget at what point I said, "No, pull it up. It's better to concentrate than expand." The next-to-last story in *Nobel Rot* ("La Pourriture Noble") was beginning to swell, and I didn't want it to. I wanted to concentrate. I think most writers have a preferred length. Bellow has swollen his things with essays because he desires to comment on everything, and he's good at it. He has so much poetic and intellectual energy that he bewitches you. I think his best form is the novella, *Seize the Day*, *Him with His Foot in His Mouth*, though *Herzog* is magnificent. Of course, *Humboldt* and *Augie March* are also wonderful. So where am I?

Schiffer: You've been called a master of the short story.

Stern: I learned early how to pack a lot of story up front, to start with an explosion and then work it out. I also think I can do a short novel pretty well. I can't do a big novel. I don't know how to handle it. I just don't feel right with it.

Schiffer: I'm fascinated by the portraiture motif in *Natural Shocks*, the character who captures others in words, the character who gets captured, who reads about his reduced self. The theme is in *A Father's Words* too, the caricatured version of Riemer – as a philandering doctor – in son Jack's television show.

Stern: Right. The theme goes back at least as far as Poppa Hondorp getting golked in *Golk*. It's clear that putting the world into words has strange consequences. Anybody in this business and anybody, I suppose, in the TV business is assailed by problems involved in it. "Boy, do I have a story to tell you!" From that to "What's it like for me to be exposed, revealed?" Even in *Other Men's Daughters* the way the family finds out about the affair is that *Newsweek* publishes a little story about the brush fire in France and mentions Cynthia and Merriwether. The way the exposure and publicity can change your life and change you into a version – a smaller version – of yourself. Then you keep wondering, "Am I doing this to other people?" Inevitably. For what purpose? What's the payment?

Schiffer: After he sees the version of himself on television, Riemer says to his son Jack that he understands why Jack modeled his characters on people he knows and feels strongly about. But, Riemer adds, "I just wish you didn't feel about me the way it shows up." Has anyone ever said this to you?

Stern: My oldest son, Christopher, and I have had a lot of discussions. He said after *A Father's Words*, "I realized how little you understood me after I read that book." Well, I said, "It's not just you." You know the process. I used that Conrad quote in my essay on autobiographical fiction, "Inside Narcissus" [in *The Invention of the Real*, 1982]: Conrad said our real lives go on in other people's heads. I still have to answer for writing about people.

Schiffer: How innovative is your fiction?

Stern: After *1968* Giles Gordon, a minor English writer who became an editor, told me that a lot of English writers – probably three – thought that I was an experimental writer. I wonder. I shied away from the *outré* or sheer kicks. I remember arguing with [John] Barth, who doesn't think I'm an artist at all. "Oh, you know a lot, and you've got energy," he says. "But where's the virtuosity? Where's the art?" I can't answer that.

Schiffer: What have been the most important influences on you as a writer?

Stern: [Stendhal's] *The Red and the Black* was a big influence. Proust means so much to me. Ford Madox Ford's *The Good Soldier*. Influences? James. Dante. Bellow. He's someone who keeps going, who's disciplined. I admire that. And to keep going at 73. I can already feel . . . I've had a flirtation or two with extinction. Life readies you for not living.

Notes and References

Chapter One

1. *The Invention of the Real* (Athens: University of Georgia Press, 1982), 233; hereafter cited in text as *IR*.

2. Roger Flaherty, "Richard Stern Captures *Sun-Times* Book Award," *Chicago Sun-Times*, 21 January 1990; hereafter cited in text.

3. When the award was made there were 15 books. *Shares and Other Fictions* (Harrison, N.Y.: Delphinium, 1992), the sixteenth, contains Stern's eighth novel, *Shares: A Novel in Ten Pieces*; the volume also contains four stories and a novella and is thus his fifth story collection as well. *Shares and Other Fictions* is hereafter cited in text as *Shares*.

4. Mark Harris, Introduction to *Other Men's Daughters* (New York: Arbor House, 1986), xiv.

5. David Kubal, review of *Packages*, *Hudson Review* 34 (Autumn 1981): 459.

6. James Atlas, "The Art of Fiction: Richard Stern," *Paris Review* (forthcoming); hereafter cited in text.

7. Henry George Stern, *Reminiscences of a Gentle Man* (New York: privately published, 1979); in the Dr. Albert Berg Collection, New York Public Library.

8. "Penned In," *Critical Inquiry* 13 (Fall 1986): 10; hereafter cited in text.

9. "In Response to a Questionnaire," *The Books In Fred Hampton's Apartment* (New York: Dutton, 1973), 143; hereafter cited in text as *FH*.

10. See also Bonnie Birtwistle and James Schiffer, "Stern Talks about Writing," *Chicago*, June 1978, 184; hereafter cited in text.

11. "Wissler Remembers" is included in two Stern collections: *Packages* (New York: Coward, McCann & Geoghegan, 1980) and *Noble Rot: Stories, 1949-1988* (New York: Grove Press, 1989). *Noble Rot* is hereafter cited in text as *NR*.

12. *Europe: Or Up and Down with Schreiber and Baggish* (New York: McGraw-Hill, 1961); republished with corrected title as *Europe: Or Up and Down with Baggish and Schreiber* (London: Macgibbon & Kee, 1962). In most of Stern's subsequent listings, the title is presented as *Europe, or Up and Down with Baggish and Schreiber*. Hereafter cited in text as *Europe*.

13. Paul Engle and Hansford Martin, eds., *Prize Stories of 1954: The O. Henry Collection* (Garden City, N.Y.: Doubleday, 1954).

14. "American Poetry of the Fifties," *Western Review* 21 (Spring 1957): 164-238.

15. "Hip, Hell and the Navigator," *Western Review* 23 (Spring 1959): 101-9; republished in *Advertisements for Myself*, by Norman Mailer (New York: Putnam's, 1959).

16. *Honey and Wax: Pleasures and Powers of Narrative*, illustrated by Joan FitzGerald (Chicago: University of Chicago Press, 1968).

17. *The Position of the Body* (Evanston, Ill.: Northwestern University Press, 1986), 129; hereafter cited in text as *PB*.

18. *Golk* (New York: Criterion, 1960; paperback reprint, Chicago: University of Chicago Press, Phoenix Fiction, 1987); hereafter cited in text. *In Any Case* (New York: McGraw-Hill, 1962); republished as *The Chaleur Network* (Sagaponac, N.Y.: Second Chance Press, 1981). *In Any Case/The Chaleur Network* is hereafter cited in text as *CN*. *Teeth, Dying and Other Matters* (New York: Harper & Row, 1964); hereafter cited in text as *Teeth*. *Stitch* (New York: Harper & Row, 1965; paperback reprint, New York: Arbor House, 1986); hereafter cited in text.

19. "On Reprinting *Golk*," *Agni Review* 26 (1988): 31; hereafter cited in text as "On *Golk*."

20. Jean Overton Fuller, *Double Webs* (New York: Putnam's, 1958).

21. Stern has published three nonfiction accounts of the incident, each slightly different from the other two: "Pound Sterling," *FH*, 291-92; "A Memory or Two of Pound," *IR*, 5-7; "Journal," *IR*, 157.

22. *1968: A Short Novel, An Urban Idyll, Five Stories, and Two Trade Notes* (New York: Holt, Rinehart & Winston, 1970); hereafter cited in text as *1968*.

23. *Other Men's Daughters* (New York: Dutton, 1973; paperback reprint, New York: Arbor House, 1986); hereafter cited in text as *OMD*.

24. *Natural Shocks* (New York: Coward, McCann & Geoghegan, 1978; paperback reprint, New York: Arbor House, 1986); hereafter cited in text as *NS*.

25. *A Father's Words* (New York: Arbor House, 1986; paperback reprint, Chicago: University of Chicago Press, Phoenix Fiction, 1990); hereafter cited in text as *FW*.

26. *Noble Rot* was republished in paperback by Another Chicago Press (Chicago) in 1993.

27. *One Person and Another* was to be published by Baskerville Press (Dallas) in 1993.

28. Letter to James Schiffer, 11 March 1991.

29. "The Actions of an Innocent Person," *Chicago Tribune*, 15 October 1991, 17; "Up Close, in Person, Wimbledon a Marvel," *Chicago Tribune*, 28 June 1992, Sports Section.

30. John Seelye, review of *Noble Rot*, *Chicago*, January 1989, 83.

31. Douglas Unger, Introduction to *Natural Shocks* (New York: Arbor House, 1986), iii.

32. Doris Grumbach, review of *A Father's Words*, *Chicago Tribune Book World*, 6 April 1986, 40.

Chapter Two

1. Elliott Anderson and Milton Rosenberg, "A Conversation with Richard Stern," *Chicago Review* 31 (Winter 1980): 104; hereafter cited in text.

2. Joan Didion, review of *Golk*, *National Review*, 7 May 1960, 306; Anthony Burgess, dust jacket quote, *Natural Shocks* (1978); Stephen Donadio, review of *Teeth, Dying and Other Matters*, *Partisan Review* 32 (Spring 1965): 299; Thomas Berger, dust jacket quote, *The Books in Fred Hampton's Apartment*; review of *1968*, *Times Literary Supplement*, 21 May 1971, 581; James Marcus, review of *Noble Rot*, *Village Voice Literary Supplement*, April 1989, 24.

3. John Gardner, *The Art of Fiction* (New York: Vintage, 1985), 31. Stern has apparently never read this book by Gardner.

4. In a note Stern adds that "the result was a short novel which did exhibit its process (*Veni, Vidi . . . Wendt*) and a novel which was reduced to a long story ('Idylls of Dugan and Strunk')," both published in *1968* (*FH*, 142).

5. Frank MacShane, Introduction to *Stitch* (New York: Arbor House, 1986), x.

6. D. A. N. Jones, review of *1968*, *New York Review of Books*, 13 August 1970, 26.

7. See also my interview with Stern in the Appendix; hereafter cited in text as Appendix.

8. Philip Roth, dust jacket quote, *Natural Shocks* (1986).

9. Sven Birkerts, "Chekhov in Chicago," review of *Noble Rot*, *New Republic*, 20 February 1989, 47; hereafter cited in text.

10. Bernard F. Rodgers, Jr., Foreword to *Golk* (Chicago: University of Chicago Press, 1987), vii; hereafter cited in text.

11. Review of *Noble Rot*, *Kirkus Reviews*, 1 November 1988, 1561; hereafter cited in text as *Kirkus*.

12. John Bowers, review of *A Father's Words*, *New York Times Book Review*, 15 June 1986, 15. The Tolstoy comparison originates with protag-

onist Cyrus Riemer, who notes that he (Riemer) and Tolstoy were born on the same day in August, in 1828 and 1928.

13. Peter S. Prescott, review of *A Father's Words*, *Newsweek*, 24 March 1986, 74; hereafter cited in text.

14. Marcus Klein, "Richard Stern," *Contemporary Novelists*, 4th ed., ed. D. L. Kirkpatrick (New York: St. Martin's Press, 1986), 781.

15. Molly McQuade, "PW Interviews: Richard Stern," *Publisher's Weekly*, 20 January 1989, 126; hereafter cited in text.

16. Mark Harris, review of *Packages*, *New Republic*, 15 November 1980, 33.

17. Richard Ellmann, dust jacket quote, *The Books in Fred Hampton's Apartment*.

18. The *Manchester Guardian* quote is used on the dust jacket of *A Father's Words*.

19. James R. Frakes, review of *Other Men's Daughters*, *New York Times Book Review*, 18 November 1973, 5; hereafter cited in text.

20. Jean W. Ross, "STERN, Richard (Gustave)," *Contemporary Authors*, new revision series, vol. 25, ed. Hal May and Deborah A. Straub (Detroit: Gale, 1989), 430.

21. Letter to James Schiffer, 6 March 1992.

22. Tom Rogers, review of *Noble Rot*, *Chicago Sun-Times Book Week*, 29 January 1989; hereafter cited in text.

Chapter Three

1. Jim Spencer, "Novel Honor," *Chicago Tribune*, 25 April 1985, 5, 4-5.

2. In "On Reprinting *Golk*" Stern describes his subsequent correspondence with Funt about the possibility of a film about "Candid Camera" based on *Golk*; after reading the novel Funt was against the idea (33-34).

3. "Pound as Translator," *Accent* 13 (Autumn 1953): 265-68.

4. See interview in the Appendix for a less confident view of Pound.

5. Karl Shapiro, dust jacket quote, *Stitch* (1986); Hugh Kenner, "Stitch: The Master's Voice," *Chicago Review* 18 (Winter-Spring 1966): 176-80; hereafter cited in text.

6. Robert L. Raeder, "An Interview with Richard G. Stern," *Chicago Review* 18 (Winter-Spring 1966): 175; hereafter cited in text. See also interview in the Appendix.

Chapter Four

1. An earlier version of this scene was published as "The Beautiful Widow and the Bakery Girl," in *Literary Outtakes*, ed. Larry Dark (New York: Ballentine, 1990), 168-71.

2. John P. Sisk, review of *Europe: Or Up and Down with Baggish and Schreiber*, *New York Times Book Review*, 12 November 1961, 55.

3. Published without attribution to Stern, the article appeared under the subheading "Gaps" in the section "Commonwealth Avenue," in *Bostonia*, March-April 1991, 9-10; hereafter cited in text as *Bostonia*.

4. See "Afternoons with the Grand Jacques," *London Review of Books*, 15 August 1991, 20-21; hereafter cited in text as "Derrida."

5. See "Scanning American Poetry: 1947-1987," *The World & I*, February 1988, 691-701. See also interview in the Appendix.

Chapter Five

1. There is also some resemblance between Herbert Hondorp of *Golk* and Reg Share (and Jack Riemer).

2. See *Golk*, 50, and *Stitch*, 19.

3. *Veni, Vidi . . . Wendt* first appeared in the *Paris Review* in 1970 and was also published that same year in *1968*. In addition, Stern has included the novella in *Shares and Other Fictions* (1992). All citations are to the 1992 (Delphinium) edition.

Chapter Six

1. Robert Casillo, *The Genealogy of Demons: Anti-Semitism, Fascism, and the Myths of Ezra Pound* (Evanston, Ill.: Northwestern University Press, 1988); see also the interview in the Appendix.

Chapter Seven

1. Peter Buitenhuis, review of *In Any Case*, *New York Times Book Review*, 14 October 1962, 5.

2. Frederick Crews, review of *Teeth, Dying and Other Matters*, *New York Review of Books*, 22 October 1964, 7.

3. Edward Gunther makes his debut as a character in "Orvieto Dominos, Bolsena Eels" in *Teeth, Dying and Other Matters* in 1964, and he also appears in "Recital for the Pope" (published in *Packages* in 1980 but probably drafted in the early 1960s). Significantly, Gunther is unmarried in these two stories, while in *Stitch* he is married and has three children.

4. Granville Hicks, review of *Teeth, Dying and Other Matters*, *Saturday Review*, 12 December 1964, 35.

5. Stern had actually been invited by an editor at *Harper's* to write a review of several books on death; Stern never completed the assignment (Anderson, 100).

6. Some of the feelings for Cicia (not the amorous ones) may involve a transference of Stern's grief about his close friend and colleague Arthur

Heiserman, who died of cancer at 46 in 1977. *Natural Shocks* is dedicated
to Heiserman, and Stern creates a version of his friend in the character of
Will Eddy.

Chapter Eight

1. Stern's children were born in the following order: Christopher
(1951), Kate (1952), Andrew (1957), and Nicholas (1961). In *Stitch* the
Gunthers have three children: son Brose (11), daughter Cammie (10), and
baby son Quentin. In *Veni, Vidi . . . Wendt* the Wendts have four children:
Jeff-U (17), Gina (16), Davy (preteen), and Gus (small child). In *Other Men's
Daughters* the Merriwethers have four children: Albie (in college), Priscilla
(about to attend college), Esmé (12), and George (5 or 6). In *Natural
Shocks* the Wursups have two college-age sons, Billy and Petey. In *A
Father's Words* Agnes and Cyrus Riemer have four children: Jenny (30+),
Jack (30+), Ben (25+), and Livy (25+).

2. After writing this chapter I read Joseph Coates's wonderfully perceptive review of *Shares and Other Fictions* in the *Chicago Tribune Book
World* (6 September 199, 4). Coates discusses the "Laius Complex" in
Stern's fiction: "the tendency of fathers to make life as hazardous as possible for sons, to leave them as infants on some psychic or actual hillside."

Chapter Nine

1. "Some Members of the Congress," *Critical Inquiry* 14 (Summer
1988): 860-91; hereafter cited in text.

2. Joyce Carol Oates, "Response to Richard Stern," *Critical Inquiry* 15
(Autumn 1988): 193-95. Along with her letter, Oates sent a photograph of
herself to correct the impression created by Stern's portrait. Stern's
response to Oates appears in the same issue: "The portrait Ms. Oates sent to
Critical Inquiry is at odds with that in the piece. The person revealed in
her letter is at odds with both" (195).

3. Hugh Kenner, publisher's reader report (1992) on *One Person and
Another*; quoted with permission.

4. I owe a debt here to Scott Colley whose impressions of Stern's Derrida essay helped shape my own.

5. Letter to James Schiffer, 19 September 1991.

6. When I mentioned to Stern the similarity, he replied, "Ah, but Fenchal's portrait of Wursup is inaccurate. Mine of Oates isn't" (telephone
conversation, 15 August 1992).

Chapter Ten

1. Philip Roth, advertisement for *1968*, *New York Times*, 8 July 1970,
41.

2. *Other Men's Daughters* was also attacked for depicting sexual relations between a married professor and a student in a moralistic essay by "Aristides" (Joseph Epstein, a former student of Stern's) in *American Scholar* 44 (Summer 1975): 357-63.

3. "Scanning American Poetry: 1947-1987," 691-701; see also interview in the Appendix.

4. Susan Braudy, review of *Other Men's Daughters*, *Ms.*, March 1974, 39.

5. Stern's comments come from "Old Humanists & New," which had been scheduled for publication in *Encounter* (October 1990); that journal ceased publication before the essay could appear. "Old Humanists & New" is included in Stern's latest collection, *One Person and Another*. Hereafter cited in text as "Old Humanists."

6. Stern's review of *Catch-22* is included in *The Books in Fred Hampton's Apartment* (258-59); the review originally appeared in the *New York Times Book Review*, 22 October 1961, 50.

Appendix

1. One of the lectures on Pound that Jerome McGann delivered at the University of Chicago appears as "The Cantos of Ezra Pound, the Truth in Contradiction," *Critical Inquiry* 15 (1988): 1-25.

2. Jacques Derrida, "Like the Sound of the Deep Sea within a Shell: Paul de Man's War," *Critical Inquiry* 14 (1988): 590-652.

3. Gore Vidal, "How to Take Back Our Country," *Nation*, 4 June 1988, 781-83.

Selected Bibliography

PRIMARY WORKS

Novels

Europe: Or Up and Down with Schreiber and Baggish. New York: McGraw-Hill, 1961. Republished as *Europe: Or Up and Down with Baggish and Schreiber.* London: Macgibbon & Kee, 1962.

A Father's Words. New York: Arbor House, 1986. Paperback reprint, Chicago: University of Chicago Press, Phoenix Fiction, 1990.

Golk. New York: Criterion, 1960. Paperback reprint, Chicago: University of Chicago Press, Phoenix Fiction, 1987.

In Any Case. New York: McGraw-Hill, 1962. Republished as *The Chaleur Network.* Sagaponack, N.Y.: Second Chance Press, 1981.

Natural Shocks. New York: Coward, McCann & Geoghegan, 1978. Paperback reprint, New York: Arbor House, 1986.

Other Men's Daughters. New York: Dutton, 1973. Paperback reprint, New York: Arbor House, 1986.

Stitch. New York: Harper & Row, 1965. Paperback reprint, New York: Arbor House, 1986.

Collected Short Fiction

1968: A Short Novel, An Urban Idyll, Five Stories, and Two Trade Notes. New York: Holt, Rinehart & Winston, 1970.

Noble Rot: Stories, 1949-1988. New York: Grove Press, 1989. Paperback reprint, Chicago: Another Chicago Press, 1993.

Packages. New York: Coward, McCann & Geoghegan, 1980.

Shares and Other Fictions. Harrison, N.Y.: Delphinium, 1992.

Teeth, Dying and Other Matters. New York: Harper & Row, 1964.

Collected Nonfiction

The Books in Fred Hampton's Apartment. New York: Dutton, 1973.

The Invention of the Real. Athens: University of Georgia Press, 1982.

One Person and Another. Dallas: Baskerville Press, in press.

The Position of the Body. Evanston, Ill.: Northwestern University Press, 1986.

Edited Volumes

"American Poetry of the Fifties." *Western Review* 21 (Spring 1957): 164-238.

Honey and Wax: Pleasures and Powers of Narrative. Illustrated by Joan FitzGerald. Chicago: University of Chicago Press, 1968.

Uncollected Essays

"The Actions of an Innocent Person." *Chicago Tribune*, 15 October 1991, 17.

"Samuel Beckett." *Salmagundi* 90-91 (Spring-Summer 1991): 179-90.

"Gaps" [published without attribution to Stern]. *Bostonia*, March-April 1991, 9-10.

"Hip, Hell and the Navigator." *Western Review* 23 (Spring 1959): 101-9; republished in *Advertisements for Myself*, by Norman Mailer, New York: Putnam's, 1959.

"Lillian Hellman on Her Plays." *Contact* 3 (1959): 113-19.

"Missingeria and Literary Health." *Georgia Review* 34 (Summer 1980): 422-27.

"On Reprinting *Golk.*" *Agni Review* 26 (1988): 31-34.

"Penned In." *Critical Inquiry* 13 (Fall 1986): 1-32.

"Scanning American Poetry: 1947-1987." *The World & I*, February 1988, 691-701.

"Several Afternoons with the Grand Jacques." *London Review of Books*, 15 August 1991, 20-21.

"Some Members of the Congress." *Critical Inquiry* 14 (Summer 1988): 860-91.

"That Same Pain, That Same Pleasure: An Interview with Ralph Ellison." *December* 3 (Winter 1961): 30-46; republished in *Shadow and Act*, by Ralph Ellison, New York: Random House, 1963.

"This Is the Way It Was." *Salmagundi* 78-79 (Spring-Summer 1988): 220-27.

"Up Close, in Person, Wimbledon a Marvel." *Chicago Tribune* 28 June 1992, Sports Section.

SECONDARY WORKS

Interviews

Anderson, Elliott, and Milton Rosenberg. "A Conversation with Richard Stern." *Chicago Review* 31 (Winter 1980): 98-108.

Atlas, James. "The Art of Fiction: Richard Stern." *Paris Review*, forthcoming.

Birtwistle, Bonnie, and James Schiffer. "Stern Talks about Writing." *Chicago*, June 1978, 184-90.

Brooks, David. "Richard Stern in Conversation with David Brooks." *Phoenix Review* 6 (Spring/Summer 1990): 47-57.

Coburn, Marcia Froelke. "Writer Takes Hard Look at Brick Wall." *Chicago Sun-Times*, 20 November 1983, Living Section, 3.

McQuade, Molly. "PW Interviews: Richard Stern." *Publishers Weekly*, 20 January 1989, 126-28.

Raeder, Robert L. "An Interview with Richard Stern." *Chicago Review* 18 (Winter-Spring 1966): 170-75.

Rima, Larry. "An Interview with Richard Stern." *Chicago Review* 28 (Winter 1977): 145-48.

Ross, Jean W. "STERN, Richard (Gustave)." *Contemporary Authors*, new revision series, vol. 25, edited by Hal May and Deborah A. Straub. Detroit: Gale Research, 1989.

Articles and Reviews

Braudy, Susan. "Man in the Middle." Review of *Other Men's Daughters*. *Ms.*, March 1974, 39-40.

Birkerts, Sven. "Chekhov in Chicago." Review of *Noble Rot*. *New Republic*, 20 February 1989, 46-48.

Buitenhuis, Peter. Review of *In Any Case*. *New York Times Book Review*, 14 October 1962, 5.

Coates, Joseph. Review of *Shares and Other Fictions*. *Chicago Tribune Book World*, 6 September 1992, 4.

Crews, Frederick. Review of *Teeth, Dying and Other Matters*. *New York Review of Books*, 22 October 1964, 7.

Frakes, James R. Review of *Other Men's Daughters*. *New York Times Book Review*, 18 November 1973, 4-5.

Gross, John. Review of *A Father's Words*. *New York Times*, 11 April 1986, 21.

Harris, Mark. "The Art of Being Brief." Review of *Packages*. *New Republic*, 15 November 1980, 32-34.

——. Introduction to *Other Men's Daughters*. New York: Arbor House, 1986.

Jones, D. A. N. Review of *1968*. *New York Review of Books*, 13 August 1970, 26.

Kenner, Hugh. "Stitch: The Master's Voice." Review of *Stitch*. *Chicago Review* 18 (Winter-Spring 1966): 176-80.

Klein, Marcus. "Richard Stern." In *Contemporary Novelists* 4th ed., edited by D. L. Kirkpatrick. New York: St. Martin's Press, 1986.

Kubal, David. Review of *Packages*. *Hudson Review* 34 (Autumn 1981): 458-59.

MacShane, Frank. Introduction to *Stitch*. New York: Arbor House, 1986.

Oates, Joyce Carol. "Response to Richard Stern." *Critical Inquiry* 15 (Autumn 1988): 193-95.

Rodgers, Jr., Bernard F. Foreword to *Golk*. Chicago: University of Chicago Press, 1987.

Rogers, Tom. "Stern's Rowdy Maelstroms of Short Stories." Review of *Noble Rot*. *Chicago Sun-Times Book Week*, 29 January 1989.

Rojo, Rodolfo. "Vigencia del realismo como modo literario: estrategias narrativas en dos novelas de Richard G. Stern." *Revista Chilena de Literatura* 14 (1979): 129-39.

Schiffer, James. "Richard Stern." In *Dictionary of Literary Biography Yearbook: 1987*, edited by J. M. Brook. Detroit: Gale Research, 1988.

Sisk, John P. Review of *Europe: Or Up and Down with Baggish and Schreiber*. *New York Times Book Review*, 12 November 1961, 55.

Southern, Terry. Review of *Golk*. *Nation*, 7 May 1960, 407.

Spencer, Jim. "Novel Honor." *Chicago Tribune*, 25 April 1985, Section 5.

Unger, Douglas. Introduction to *Natural Shocks*. New York: Arbor House, 1986.

Books

Harris, Mark. *Saul Bellow, Drumlin Woodchuck*. Athens: University of Georgia Press, 1980.

Stern, Henry George. *Reminiscences of a Gentle Man*. New York: privately published, 1978.

Index

12, 113, 118, 131-32, 137,
144, 147, 149, 150, 151, 153
"storymaking," 9, 96-97
style, Stern's, 19-30, 148-49
Sulzberger, C. L., 129
Swenson, May, 5

Tate, Allen, 27
Taylor, Peter, 21
Teeth, Dying and Other Matters,
7, 8, 11, 19, 90, 92, 150
"Teeth," 9, 14, 26, 27, 59-60, 64,
72, 90, 150
Thomas, Clarence, 13, 144
Tolstoy, Leo, 23, 24; *Anna
Karenina*, 35; *War and
Peace*, 44
"Troubles," 11, 72-73, 150
Twain, Mark, 52

"Underway," 20
Unger, Douglas, 14
Updike, John, 21, 108, 148, 155
Van Gogh, Vincent, 138
Veni, Vidi . . . Wendt, 9, 12, 14,
15, 21, 46, 67-68, 83, 93, 94,

95, 96, 98, 111, 112, 114, 118,
137, 151, 155
Vidal, Gore, 153

Wagner, Richard, 55, 140
Walpole, Horace, 95
"Wanderers," 9, 15, 60-61, 64,
72, 90, 150
Warhol, Andy, 135
Warren, Robert Penn, 27
West, Nathaneal, 19
Wilmot, John (Earl of
Rochester), 68, 69
"Wissler Remembers," 5, 11, 14,
28
Wolff, Tobias, 21
women, Stern's depiction of, 11,
36-38, 59-61, 70, 72-73, 129,
141-42, 149-50
"writer's writer," Stern as, 1, 13-
14, 18

"Zhoof," 11-12, 15, 55-56, 73-74,
88-89, 93, 140, 144, 152-53,
154
Zwerin, Michael, 155

The Author

James Schiffer is associate professor and chair of the English Department at Hampden-Sydney College in Virginia. After receiving his B.A. from the University of Pennsylvania in 1973, he earned his M.A. (1974) and Ph.D. (1980) in English at the University of Chicago. His work has appeared in such journals as *Chicago Review, Modern Philology, Chicago,* and the *South Carolina Review,* and such volumes as *The Dictionary of Literary Biography Yearbook: 1987.* His essay "*Macbeth* and the Bearded Women" appeared in *In Another Country: Feminist Perspectives on Renaissance Drama,* ed. Susan Baker and Dorothea Kehler (1991). As "Susan James," he and his wife, Susan, coauthored the academic mystery novel *Foul Deeds* (1989).

The Editor

Frank Day is a professor of English at Clemson University. He is the author of *Sir William Empson: An Annotated Bibliography* and *Arthur Koestler: A Guide to Research*. He was a Fulbright Lecturer in American Literature in Romania (1980-81) and in Bangladesh (1986-87).